Answers to
Essential
Questions
About Standards,
Assessments,
Grading, & Reporting

RELATED TITLES FROM CORWIN BY THOMAS R. GUSKEY AND LEE ANN JUNG

Answers to
Essential
Questions

About Standards,
Assessments,
Grading, & Reporting

Thomas R. Guskey
Lee Ann Jung

CORWIN
A SAGE Company

CORWIN
A SAGE Company

FOR INFORMATION:

Corwin
A SAGE Company
2455 Teller Road
Thousand Oaks, California 91320
(800) 233-9936
www.corwin.com

SAGE Publications Ltd.
1 Oliver's Yard
55 City Road
London EC1Y 1SP
United Kingdom

SAGE Publications India Pvt. Ltd.
B 1/I 1 Mohan Cooperative Industrial Area
Mathura Road, New Delhi 110 044
India

SAGE Publications Asia-Pacific Pte. Ltd.
3 Church Street
#10-04 Samsung Hub
Singapore 049483

Copyright © 2013 by Corwin

Printed in the United States of America

Library of Congress Cataloging-in-Publication Data

Guskey, Thomas R.

Answers to essential questions about standards, assessments, grading, and reporting / Thomas R. Guskey, Lee Ann Jung.

p. cm.
Includes bibliographical references and index.

ISBN 978-1-4522-3524-0 (pbk.)

1. Education—Standards—United States.
2. Grading and marking (Students)—United States.
I. Jung, Lee Ann. II. Title.

LB3060.83.G87 2013
379.1'58—dc23   2012025689

This book is printed on acid-free paper.

Acquisitions Editor: Dan Alpert
Associate Editor: Megan Bedell
Editorial Assistant: Heidi Arndt
Permissions Editor: Karen Ehrmann
Project Editor: Veronica Stapleton
Copy Editor: Terri Lee Paulsen
Typesetter: C&M Digitals (P) Ltd.
Proofreader: Dennis W. Webb
Indexer: Molly Hall
Cover Designer: Anupama Krishnan

SUSTAINABLE FORESTRY INITIATIVE

Certified Chain of Custody
Promoting Sustainable Forestry
www.sfiprogram.org
SFI-01268

SFI label applies to text stock

12 13 14 15 16 10 9 8 7 6 5 4 3 2 1

Contents

Acknowledgments

C orwin gratefully acknowledges the contributions of the following reviewers:

Jeanne Collins
Superintendent
Burlington School District
Burlington, Vermont

Kurtis Hewson
Faculty Associate
University of Lethbridge
Alberta, Canada

Frederick Holmes
Redesign Lead Teacher
Manassas High School
Memphis, Tennessee

Nancy Kellogg
Education Consultant
Boulder, Colorado

Kevin King
Assessment Development Coordinator
Utah State Office of Education
Salt Lake City, Utah

Terry Morganti-Fisher
Educational Consultant
Learning Forward and QLD Learning
Austin, Texas

Julie Quinn
Accountability Specialist
Utah State Office of Education
Salt Lake City, Utah

Sharon Tritschler
National Facilitator, NSRF
NCAC Career Academy Review Coordinator
Osprey, Florida

Nancy Wyngaard
Director of Professional Development and Special Programs
Middleton–Cross Plains Area Schools
Middleton, Wisconsin

About the Authors

Thomas R. Guskey, PhD, is Professor of Educational Psychology in the College of Education at the University of Kentucky. A graduate of the University of Chicago, he began his career in education as a middle school teacher, served as an administrator in Chicago Public Schools, and was the first director of the *Center for the Improvement of Teaching and Learning,* a national educational research center. He is the author/editor of 18 books and over 200 published articles. Dr. Guskey served on the Policy Research Team of the *National Commission on Teaching & America's Future,* on the Task Force to develop the *National Standards for Staff Development,* and in 2009 was named a fellow in the American Educational Research Association, which also honored him in 2006 for his outstanding contribution relating research to practice. His most recent books include *Benjamin S. Bloom: Portraits of an Educator* (2nd ed.) (2012), *Developing Standards-Based Report Cards* (with J. Bailey) (2010), *Practical Solutions for Serious Problems in Standards-Based Grading* (Ed.) (2009), *The Principal as Assessment Leader* (Ed.) (2009), and *The Teacher as Assessment Leader* (Ed.) (2009).

Lee Ann Jung, PhD, is an associate professor of special education at the University of Kentucky. Dr. Jung is a graduate of Auburn University and has worked in the field of special education since 1994 as a teacher, administrator, consultant, and researcher. She is a national presenter on topics of family involvement, inclusion, IEP/ IFSP development, and grading and reporting progress of exceptional learners. She has authored more than 30 journal articles and book chapters and has received in excess of $3 million in funding to support personnel preparation and research. She is an editorial board member for three special education journals and has served as guest editor for *Topics in Early Childhood Special Education*. Dr. Jung was named Outstanding Junior Faculty Researcher at the University of Kentucky in 2002. She serves on the governor-appointed council that advises Kentucky's Cabinet for Health and Family Services on matters of providing special education services to young children. Dr. Jung was lead author with Dr. Guskey on *Grading Exceptional and Struggling Learners* (2012), which was a finalist for the 2012 Distinguished Achievement Award by the Association of Educational Publishers.

Preface

The Nature of Essential Questions

Educators today are under great pressure to make improvements. Government officials and policy makers regularly proclaim that the vast majority of students are not adequately prepared to succeed in college or careers in the 21st century, and drastic change in education is needed. These same officials often go so far as to prescribe the changes educators should make. In most cases they focus on *standards, assessments, grading,* and *reporting.* These four areas provide the foundation for nearly every modern education reform initiative. Yet despite how frequently these areas are mentioned in discussions of education reform, it's not always clear just what each means. Rarer still are specific ideas about the changes in each area that will bring about the desired improvements.

Making matters even more complicated is the tendency of educators, when a particular idea or strategy is not working very well, simply to change its name. In other words, we seldom change ideas substantively; we merely re-label them. When educators grew frustrated with certain aspects of *testing,* for example, believing that it undermined instructional purposes and detracted from learning, teachers and school leaders abandoned the term. Today, few educators would admit to doing any amount of testing. Instead, we have *assessments.*

Similarly, for years educators struggled with the use of *essay questions.* They were time-consuming for teachers to develop and difficult to score objectively. So today, teachers as well as assessment manufacturers have abandoned the use of essay questions. Instead, we have *open-ended, constructed-response*, and *extended response* questions.

Our tendency simply to *change the name* has resulted in a tangled thicket of terminology in education that detracts from serious improvement efforts. This became evident to us several years ago when we were asked to work with the members of a school district's curriculum development committee who were stalled in their efforts to design a new districtwide curriculum. We quickly discovered that what prevented committee members from making significant progress were squabbles over terminology. These thoughtful, dedicated, and highly knowledgeable educators spent most of their time arguing about the differences in *standards, goals*, and *objectives*.

To help them get past this hurdle and avoid continued frustration, we wrote a simple statement on a single sheet of paper. Our statement began with the phrase, "The student will be able to . . ." We then added a popular, high-level, performance-based verb such as *demonstrate,* and completed the statement with some elements of content. We showed our statement to the group and asked them to consider it a simple, multiple-choice question. "Please read this statement," we asked, "and tell us, is this statement a(n):

a. Objective

b. Goal

c. Standard

d. Outcome

e. Target

f. Benchmark

g. Competency

h. Proficiency

i. Performance

j. Expectation

k. Aspiration

l. New Year's Resolution?

The resulting debate was far more serious than we ever intended and took up most of the next hour. When the committee took a break, we left the room and walked to the cafeteria where students were having lunch. There we showed our statement to 10 high school students and asked them the same question. Unlike the teachers and school leaders on the curriculum development committee who had great difficulty reaching consensus, all the students we asked gave us the same answer: "Who cares?"

We certainly recognize that distinctions in terminology can be helpful, especially when they clarify issues and enable meaningful communication. But the confusion and distraction that such trivial distinctions often cause must be avoided. While it is vitally important in designing any curriculum that educators be clear about what they expect students to learn and be able to do as a result of their experiences in school, the particular label we attach to those things is immaterial.

This is but one example of the confusion and uncertainty that reigns among educators today with regard to these issues. In our work with school districts and education agencies throughout the United States and abroad, we consistently hear the same essential questions from teachers and school leaders about standards, assessments, grading, and reporting. Some of these questions deal with similarly perplexing terminology. Others reveal serious misconceptions and misunderstandings about aspects related to each area. At first glance, these essential questions may appear to be rudimentary because they deal with fundamental issues that are integral to nearly every modern education reform initiative. Nevertheless, they are questions that continue to stymie and confuse teachers and school leaders at every level of education.

In this book, we have assembled the most common and most frequently asked of these essential questions. For each question, we offer a short, simple, jargon-free, reader-friendly response that we hope makes sense to all levels of readers. Although we address our responses primarily to teachers and school leaders, we hope our readers also will include district office administrators (e.g., superintendents, curriculum and instruction specialists, professional development specialists, and assessment coordinators), parents, board of education members, community leaders, policy makers, and elected officials. As schools move forward in their improvement efforts, a shared understanding of these critical issues will not only facilitate communication among these key stakeholder groups, but it also will greatly enhance the likelihood of success.

We recognize, of course, that the issues involved with standards, assessments, grading, and reporting are much too complex and far too diverse to be addressed with simple explanations and examples. Success in reform initiatives involving these issues will depend largely on the ability of educators to approach the improvement process with sensitivity, understanding, and a true sense of purpose. Our intent, therefore, is not to offer *the one correct answer,* but rather to clarify terms and provide the basic understanding necessary to guide improvement efforts and to enable success in any context.

We also recognize that certain interpretations, and sometimes misinterpretations, of issues related to standards, assessment, grading, and reporting have led to controversy and opposition. Individuals both inside and outside of education sometimes label themselves as *anti-standards, anti-assessments,* or *anti-grading.* We believe, however, that abandoning reliance on these central aspects of modern education is neither feasible nor practical. Important considerations related to equity, quality, and efficiency make it imperative that we use these elements in thoughtful and purposeful ways. What we must do is be honest about the serious yet often unintended consequences stemming from the misuse of these elements and be more attuned to the essential characteristics of effective implementation. Having a clear understanding of these issues and a coherent vision of what they mean for education will help build capacity and support continuous improvements to help more students achieve at high levels.

Our hope for this book, as was true with our previous books, is that we do not find it sitting unread on someone's office bookshelf or in a school's professional library. Instead, we would like to see it shared by educators in schools at all levels, used and reused, analyzed and dissected. We would like to see it passed around in state departments of education, legislative committees, and board of education meetings. We hope it finds its way into undergraduate and graduate education courses to help those preparing to become teachers and experienced classroom veterans develop a deeper understanding of these important issues. It might even become the focus of study groups and faculty retreats where the answers we present to these essential questions are discussed, argued, and debated. We would like to find well-worn, coffee-stained copies of the book in teachers' lounges, with dog-eared pages and notes scribbled in the margins, where it becomes the basis for brief conversations and extended discussions.

Most important, we hope readers will take an active and reflective approach to the ideas we present. As a result, we hope it stimulates further inquiry and purposeful action. Our greatest hope, however, is that it prompts the development of higher-quality instructional programs, improved assessments, and better grading and reporting policies and practices that help educators do what they most want to accomplish: To help more students learn well, succeed in school, and gain the many positive benefits of that success.

—T. R. Guskey and L. A. Jung

PART I

Standards

1

What Are *Standards?*

Although many education programs today are said to be *standards based*, few describe just what that really means. According to *Merriam-Webster,* a standard is defined as, "something set up and established by authority as a rule for the measure of quantity, weight, extent, value, or quality" (standard, 2012). In education, we have standards covering a wide range of areas. For example, we have *Standards for Professional Preparation and Licensing* (Council for Exceptional Children, 2009), *Professional Teaching Standards* (National Board for Professional Teaching Standards, 2002), and *Standards for Professional Learning* (Learning Forward, 2011). Most conversations about standards in education today, however, involve standards for student learning.

Student learning standards are statements that describe what educators want students to learn and be able to do as a result of their experiences in school. They define the learning expectations or goals that educators strive to have students attain. As such, standards provide the foundation for every school's curriculum and instructional program.

Most academic standards include two parts. The first part describes what we want students to learn, or the *content.* This part identifies the particular knowledge, concepts, or skills that students are expected to learn. Because most elements of content are specific to a subject area, standards are generally organized by subject area. So we have standards in mathematics, language arts, science, social studies, music, art, physical education, and so forth.

In addition, because the content *within* each subject area includes a broad range of elements, documents that describe standards generally divide content elements into subtopics or "strands." The *Common Core State Standards Initiative* (National Governors Association [NGA] & Council of Chief State School Officers [CCSSO], 2010) in the United States, for example, divides the content in mathematics into six strands, shown in Figure 1.1. Individual standards are organized by grade level and grouped within each strand in order to "provide a consistent, clear understanding of what students are expected to learn, so teachers and parents know what they need to do to help them" (see http://www.corestandards.org/, p. 1).

The second part of a standard describes what we want students to be able to do, or student *behavior* in relation to the content. These behaviors can range from very simple to complex, high-level mental processes. We might, for example, want students to know specific mathematics facts related to addition and subtraction. To show they achieved this standard would require students simply to recall factual information. But we also might want students to be able to apply addition and

Figure 1.1   Content Strands in Mathematics (see http://www .corestandards.org/)

Mathematics Standards
Operations and Algebraic Thinking
Number and Operations—Base 10
Number and Operations—Fractions
Measurement and Data
Geometry
Mathematical Practices

subtraction facts in mathematics to solve complex problems in real-world situations. To show they achieved this standard would require students not only to know addition and subtraction facts, but also to use that knowledge in practical, problem-solving situations they may encounter in daily life.

Many strategies have been developed over the years to categorize different levels of student cognitive behaviors in relation to the content. One of the earliest and still widely used is Bloom's Taxonomy of Educational Objectives (Bloom, Englehart, Furst, Hill, & Krathwohl, 1956). Although other systems have been developed (e.g., Anderson & Krathwohl, 2001; Gagne, 1985; Webb, 1997), none seems as elegant or as clear. Bloom's categorization system divides student cognitive behaviors into six broad categories, ranging from simple to highly complex, as shown in Figure 1.2.

A common misunderstanding when considering these levels of behavior is to equate *complexity* with *difficulty*. Sometimes a task that requires only recall of information can be far more difficult than one that requires students to

Figure 1.2   Categories of Student Cognitive Behavior and Related Verbs (Bloom et al., 1956)

Levels of Behavior From Bloom's Taxonomy	
Behavior	*Related Verbs*
Knowledge	Tell, list, define, relate, locate, write, find, state, name
Comprehension	Explain, describe, interpret, discuss, restate, translate
Application	Solve, use, illustrate, construct, complete, examine, classify
Analysis	Analyze, examine, compare, contrast, investigate, categorize
Synthesis	Create, invent, compose, predict, plan, construct, design, devise
Evaluation	Judge, justify, debate, verify, recommend, assess, rate, prioritize

engage in higher-level reasoning. For example, asking elementary students to determine what coins they might receive in return after paying for an apple that costs 75 cents with a dollar, might prove less difficult than asking the same students to identify which term in a subtraction problem is the "subtrahend" and which is the "minuend." The first task requires the complex skill of applying mathematics facts and knowledge of currency in a practical, real-world situation. The second task requires only knowledge of a definition. Still, the second task is likely to prove more difficult for most students. Although tasks requiring more complex cognitive behaviors are generally more difficult, that is not always the case.

As expectations for student learning, most standards contain descriptions of both content and behaviors. The *Common Core State Standards for Mathematics,* for instance, includes the following standard for Grade 2 within the strand for Measurement and Data:

> 5. Use addition and subtraction within 100 to solve word problems involving lengths that are given in the same units, e.g., by using drawings (such as drawings of rulers) and equations with a symbol for the unknown number to represent the problem. (See http://www .corestandards.org/assets/CCSSI_Math%20Standards .pdf, p. 20)

This standard depicts one part of what students in Grade 2 are expected to learn and be able to do in the area of measurement and data in mathematics.

A third aspect of standards that is sometimes considered describes how well students are expected to do those things. In other words, how good is good enough? These levels of performance often include an established level of proficiency for meeting the standard, one or two levels below proficiency, and an advanced or exemplary level considered above proficiency. Setting these levels of performance can prove to be a tricky process, however.

An error frequently made in this process is to equate *level of performance* with *percent correct*. If, for example, *Proficient* is defined as answering 80% of the questions correctly on an assessment designed to measure a standard, *Advanced* or *Exemplary* should *not* mean simply answering 90% to 100% correctly or completing 100% of the tasks. If all questions relate to the same standard (e.g., solving single-digit addition problems), answering more questions correctly shows only greater accuracy. It does *not* show students' ability to work at a more advanced level or on a more advanced standard (e.g., solving double-digit addition problems). Similarly, students should not necessarily be considered less than proficient simply because they answered correctly only 70% of the questions written at the proficient level (Brookhart, 2011).

Although extremely important, these complications regarding students' level of performance relate more to how achievement of the standards is measured or assessed, rather than to the standards themselves. Note in the mathematics standard from the *Common Core* listed above that no mention is made of how well students are expected to "use addition and subtraction within 100 to solve word problems . . ." For this reason, statements about specific levels of student performance are usually absent in descriptions of standards and related curriculum documents. Instead, that becomes the focus in developing assessments to measure how well students have achieved the standards.

REFERENCES

Anderson, L. W., & Krathwohl, D. R. (Eds.). (2001). *A taxonomy for learning, teaching, and assessing: A revision of Bloom's taxonomy of educational objectives.* New York, NY: Longman.

Bloom, B. S., Englehart, M. D., Furst, E. J., Hill, W. H., & Krathwohl, D. R. (1956). *Taxonomy of educational objectives, Handbook 1: The cognitive domain.* New York, NY: McKay.

Brookhart, S. M. (2011). *Grading and learning: Practices that support student achievement.* Bloomington, IN: Solution Tree Press.

Council for Exceptional Children. (2009). *What every special educator must know: Ethics, standards, and guidelines* (6th ed., revised). Arlington, VA: Author. Retrieved from http://www.cec.sped .org/content/navigationmenu/professionaldevelopment/ professionalstandards/

Gagne, R. M. (1985). *The conditions of learning and theory of instruction.* New York, NY: CBS College Publishing.

Learning Forward. (2011). *Standards for professional learning.* Dallas, TX: Author. Retrieved from http://www.learningforward.org/ standards/index.cfm

National Governors Association (NGA) Center for Best Practices, & Council of Chief State School Officers (CCSSO). (2010). *Common core state standards initiative.* Washington, DC: Author. Retrieved from http://www.corestandards.org/assets/CCSSI_ELA%20 Standards.pdf

National Board for Professional Teaching Standards. (2002). *What teachers should know and be able to do.* Arlington, VA: Author. Retrieved from http://www.nbpts.org/UserFiles/File/what_ teachers.pdf

standard. (2012). In *Merriam-Webster.com.* Retrieved from http:// www.merriam-webster.com/dictionary/standard

Webb, N. L. (1997). *Criteria for alignment of expectations and assessments in mathematics and science education* (Research monograph No. 8). Washington, DC: Council of Chief State School Officers.

2

Are Standards a New Idea in Education?

Many people, both inside and outside of education, believe the push to define standards and clarify learning goals is a recent development in education. The dominant educational theme in recent years certainly has been to "get serious about standards" (National Commission on Teaching and America's Future, 1996, p. 2). The *Common Core State Standards Initiative* (NGA & CCSSO, 2010) in the United States renewed interest in refining the focus of educational programs by advancing specific standards for student learning in language arts and mathematics. But the importance of having well-defined learning goals is not a new idea in education. In fact, it has been recognized for decades.

Over 60 years ago, renowned educator Ralph W. Tyler (1949) stressed that prior to teaching anything to anyone, a teacher must answer two fundamental questions: (1) What do I want my students to learn and be able to do?, and (2) What evidence would I accept to verify that learning? As Tyler put it,

> If an educational program is to be planned and if efforts for continued improvement are to be made, it is necessary to have some conception of the goals being sought.

These educational objectives become the criteria by which materials are selected, content is outlined, instructional procedures are developed and tests and examinations are prepared. All aspects of the educational program are really means to accomplish these basic educational purposes. (p. 3)

Although Tyler believed that well-defined goals should drive all instructional decisions, he also emphasized that educators must continually reexamine the importance and meaning of the goals they set. Tyler further noted that a thorough examination of potential goals or standards inevitably comes down to questions about what is most valued by the organization or the individuals involved. He stressed:

In the final analysis, goals are matters of choice, and they must therefore be considered value judgments of those responsible for the school. A comprehensive philosophy of education is necessary to guide one in making these judgments. In addition, certain kinds of information and knowledge provide a more intelligent basis for applying the philosophy in making decisions about goals. If these facts are available to those making decisions, the probability is increased that judgments about goals will have greater significance and greater validity. (Tyler, 1949, p. 4)

As logical as this may seem, Tyler also pointed out that most curriculum decisions are not based on student learning goals. Instead, he maintained that they are based on *time*. We tend to worry more about what content should be covered in the time available than we do about what specific knowledge and skills students acquire. As a result, we cannot say with certainty what students who complete programs in our elementary, middle, or secondary schools have learned and are able to do. All we know for certain, argued Tyler, is how much time they spent at each school level.

Similarly at the college level, students must gain a specified number of credit hours to attain their degree. Credit hours are earned by accumulating "contact hours," which is typically defined as contact between students and their professors. From Tyler's perspective, however, credit hours more accurately reflected contact between students and their seats.

Tyler further contended that the best indicators of a teacher's effectiveness come not from what the teacher does, but from what the students are able to do. In other words, teaching and learning must be seen as intrinsically linked. For a teacher to suggest, "I taught it to them, they just didn't learn it" was to Tyler as foolish as saying, "I sold it to them, they just didn't buy it." It would be comparable to saying, "I taught this fellow to swim, even though each time he jumps in the water he still sinks." From Tyler's perspective, teaching is not something one could go off alone into the wilderness and do—not even if curriculum frameworks, textbooks, and lesson plans are carried along!

Obviously the importance of defining standards for student learning and identifying how those standards will be assessed has been recognized for many years. These are not new ideas. To improve our success in education and have more students learning better, however, we must commit ourselves to making these important decisions about the learning standards we expect students to achieve. In addition, we must clearly communicate the results of those decisions to everyone involved, and then follow through with our best efforts to help *all* students achieve those standards.

REFERENCES

National Commission on Teaching and America's Future. (1996). *What matters most: Teaching for America's future.* New York, NY: National Commission on Teaching and America's Future.

National Governors Association (NGA) Center for Best Practices, & Council of Chief State School Officers (CCSSO). (2010). *Common core state standards initiative.* Washington, DC: Author. Retrieved from http://www.corestandards.org/assets/CCSSI_ELA%20 Standards.pdf

Tyler, R. W. (1949). *Basic principles of curriculum and instruction.* Chicago, IL: University of Chicago Press.

3

Why Do Some People Oppose Standards?

Many education leaders have concerns about public opposition to standards. They fear that parents and community members might object to educators' focus on standards and the assessments used to measure students' achievement of those standards. What education leaders at all levels need to recognize, however, is that the vast majority of people in the United States, both inside and outside of education, actually support the idea of standards.

An *Education Next* poll conducted in 2007 asked whether people favored "a single national standard and a single national test for all students in the United States? Or do you think that there should be different standards and tests in different states?" The results were not even close. More than 73% of respondents wanted a single set of standards and a single test (reported in Finn & Petrilli, 2010). A more recent poll by the Association for Supervision and Curriculum Development (ASCD) showed much the same. When asked, "Will the development of national curriculum standards help your students?," 55% of respondents agreed (ASCD SmartBrief, 2011).

Those who voice opposition to standards rarely oppose the basic idea. After all, why would anyone object to educators being clear about the goals of instructional programs?

What they question are the standards themselves and who should develop them.

Difficulties in defining standards and educational goals often result because people have different philosophies of education. These philosophies reflect not only what we value as individuals, but also what we hope for and value as a society. When philosophies differ, the goals being sought differ as well. Again, Ralph W. Tyler (1949) pointed out:

> A fundamental first step in the process of defining our educational goals is to make our philosophies of schooling clear. . . . Should the school develop young people to fit into the present society as is, or does the school have a revolutionary mission to develop young people who will seek to improve the society? . . . How these questions are answered affects the educational goals we select. If the school believes its primary function is to teach people to adjust to society, it will strongly emphasize obedience to the present authorities, loyalty to the present forms and traditions, skills in carrying on the present techniques of life. Whereas if it emphasizes the revolutionary function of the school it will be more concerned with critical analysis, the ability to meet new problems, independence and self-direction, freedom, and self-discipline. (pp. 35–36)

Philosophical conflicts about how traditional or revolutionary schools should be are at the root of many current debates regarding standards. To move ahead in improvement efforts, we must make clear these differences and then work to resolve them. Only then can some degree of consensus among differing philosophical perspectives be achieved.

Related concerns about who will develop the standards stem from the American tradition of local control of schools. Because of this tradition, the United States has remained one of the few developed nations in the world *not* to have a national curriculum.

The problems associated with local control became evident in recent years with reports that showed tremendous variation in the quality and rigor of the standards set by different states (e.g., Finn, Julian, & Petrilli, 2006). Combined with evidence demonstrating that the achievement of students in the United States lagged behind that of students in other developed nations (e.g., Gonzales et al., 2008), this led to the development of the *Common Core State Standards Initiative* (NGA & CCSSO, 2010). This initiative is an effort to guarantee, for example, that the algebra that students are taught in Michigan is the same as the algebra that students are taught in Massachusetts, Mississippi, or Montana. In other words, it's an attempt to ensure equity in the quality and rigor of instructional programs, regardless of a school's location.

Philosophical debates about the purpose of education will undoubtedly persist. But while individuals may disagree on the specific standards schools should use and who should develop those standards, few will question the importance of clarifying learning goals in order to ensure quality and rigor in instructional programs for all students.

REFERENCES

ASCD SmartBrief. (2011, July 31). *Reader poll results: Will the development of national curriculum standards help your students?* Retrieved from http://www.smartbrief.com/news/ascd/poll_result.jsp? pollName=F5A022C4–5500–4F2C-AF8B-65B4C41D6FD8& issueid=703D5952-F1EB-4471–86BF-C320619DD163

Finn, C. E., Julian, L., & Petrilli, M. J. (2006). *The state of state standards.* Washington, DC: Thomas B. Fordham Foundation.

Finn, C. E., & Petrilli, M. J. (2010, July 22). The common core curriculum. *The National Review Online.* Retrieved from http://www.nationalreview.com/articles/243517/common-core-curriculum-chester-e-finn-jr?page=1

Gonzales, P., Williams, T., Jocelyn, L., Roey, S., Kastberg, D., & Brenwald, S. (2008). *Highlights from TIMSS 2007: Mathematics and science achievement of U.S. fourth- and eighth-grade students in an international context.* Washington, DC: Institute of Education Science, National Center for Education Statistics, U.S. Department of Education.

National Governors Association (NGA) Center for Best Practices, & Council of Chief State School Officers (CCSSO). (2010). *Common core state standards initiative.* Washington, DC: Author. Retrieved from http://www.corestandards.org/assets/CCSSI_ELA%20 Standards.pdf

Tyler, R. W. (1949). *Basic principles of curriculum and instruction.* Chicago, IL: University of Chicago Press.

PART II

Assessments

4

What Is *Assessment?*

A *ssessment* is one of those common terms in education that everyone uses but few people define in exactly the same way. Some educators argue that assessment is simply the more modern word for *testing*. Others contend that it implies something much more.

In the context of education, assessment is a *process* for gathering and interpreting information for use in making decisions about students, instruction, curriculums, programs, and educational policies (see American Federation of Teachers, National Council on Measurement in Education, & National Education Association, 1990).

From this definition, it is easy to see that assessment in education refers to more than simply administering, scoring, and grading tests. It includes the broad range of strategies and techniques that educators use to understand students better and to monitor the effects of instructional programs and policies. As such, assessment can certainly involve quizzes and larger examinations composed of multiple-choice and constructed-response items that are administered in pencil-and-paper form or online. But it also includes classroom observations, interviews, compositions, oral presentations, skill demonstrations, projects, reports, experiments, notebooks, journals, exhibits of students' work, and paper or digital portfolios (Russell & Airasian, 2011).

Teachers make a wide variety of decisions on the basis of assessment results. Perhaps most important, they use assessment results to determine the effectiveness of different teaching strategies, classroom activities, and instructional materials. With these data, teachers can make better decisions about what to maintain and what needs to be changed or improved. Information gathered from classroom assessments also helps teachers determine who is learning well, who is struggling, and what specific difficulties struggling students are experiencing. It gives teachers direction in developing instructional alternatives for those students who are having problems and for planning extension or enrichment activities for students who have learned well. Moreover, it allows teachers to make better decisions when planning next steps in instruction for individual students and for the entire class.

Teachers also consider assessment results when placing students into various educational programs, assigning appropriate grades, counseling students, selecting them for educational interventions or opportunities, and credentialing or certifying students' competence. Data from assessments inform decisions about the effectiveness of different curriculums and how to improve them. In addition, assessment results provide the basis for making decisions about educational policies at the classroom, school, district, state, and national levels (Nitko & Brookhart, 2010).

In essence, assessment in education is any process used to gather information about student learning; that is, what students know, are able to do, and believe at a particular point in time. In later chapters we will describe the different types of assessments and how they are used for different purposes.

REFERENCES

American Federation of Teachers, National Council on Measurement in Education, & National Education Association. (1990). *Standards for teacher competence in educational assessment of students.* Washington, DC: National Council on Measurement in

Assessments

Education. Retrieved from http://www.eric.ed.gov/PDFS/ED 323186.pdf

Nitko, A. J., & Brookhart, S. M. (2010). *Educational assessment of students* (6th ed.). Upper Saddle River, NJ: Merrill/PrenticeHall.

Russell, M. K., & Airasian, P. W. (2011). *Classroom assessment: Concepts and applications* (7th ed.). New York, NY: McGraw-Hill.

Assessments

5

What Is the Difference Between *Assessments* and *Tests?*

E veryone who has been in school has experienced a wide variety of tests. We have all seen pop quizzes, regular class quizzes, end-of-unit tests, midterm exams and, of course, final examinations. These tests were usually developed by our teachers to give them some idea of what we had learned. Most were printed on paper, although today they are increasingly administered online using computers. Sometimes our teachers used the results from these tests to tailor instructional activities in order to help us learn better. In most instances, however, results were used solely for the purpose of judging our competence and assigning grades.

Early experts defined testing broadly as, "a systematic method of sampling one or more human characteristics and the representation of these results for an individual in the form of a descriptive statement or classification" (Bloom, 1967, p. 2; also see Bloom, 1970). In other words, testing is simply an organized way of gathering and representing information about people.

Over the years, however, testing in classrooms took on a much narrower meaning. Many in education saw tests as only pencil-and-paper instruments that consisted of true–false, matching, multiple-choice, completion, and essay questions. True–false, matching, and multiple-choice questions are termed *selected-response* items because students select their response from among options that are provided. Tests composed of these types of questions have the additional advantage that they can be scored and results summarized by machines (i.e., scanning devices and computers). Completion and essay questions are considered *supply* or *constructed-response* items because students must provide their own response. Occasionally teachers assigned projects or reports to determine how well students learned. But generally, pencil-and-paper instruments or computer-administered versions of these instruments consisting of these five types of questions were the most prevalent form of testing found in classrooms at all levels of education.

In more recent times, broadening educational goals caused educators to reexamine the procedures they use to gather information on student learning. This prompted many in education to broaden their conception of testing to include a wider variety of measurement techniques. In particular, educators recognized the need to consider more varied procedures for collecting evidence on student learning.

This return to a broader conception of testing did not come simply from a desire for greater variety in response formats. Rather, it stemmed from a shared recognition among educators that many important kinds of student learning could not be measured by the selected-response items used in most large-scale standardized tests. If we want to know whether or not students have acquired some basic knowledge or can recognize an appropriate application of that knowledge, for example, then multiple-choice items offer an excellent means of gathering that information. But if we want to know how well students can organize their thoughts on a complex topic and express those thoughts to others who may be unfamiliar with the topic, then multiple-choice items are simply not adequate. Instead, students must be asked to respond through more extensive written or verbal means.

Because many important learning goals cannot be measured by selected-response items, and because many people instinctively equate the word *test* with pencil-and-paper instruments that include only these types of items, educators and measurement experts alike began using the word *assessment* to depict the broader array of measurement devices and procedures (Popham, 2011; Russell & Airasian, 2011).

So today in education, assessment describes any means educators use to gather information on student learning. It is considered a broader descriptor of the wide variety of measurement techniques educators can and should use. While assessment certainly includes paper-and-paper instruments composed of selected-response items, it also covers performances, presentations, displays, exhibits, portfolios, and other means by which students can demonstrate what they have learned and are able to do (Nitko & Brookhart, 2010; Stiggins & Chappuis, 2011). We even have *Standards for Teacher Competence in Educational Assessment of Students* (American Federation of Teachers, National Council on Measurement in Education, & National Education Association, 1990).

As we move forward with the broader definition and application of assessment procedures, however, educators must keep in mind the critical balance between accuracy and efficiency when developing assessments and interpreting results. Many measures of student achievement will continue to be based on students' responses to multiple-choice items, either in pencil-and-paper format or administered digitally, because they offer a fast and easy way to gather reliable information on a fairly broad array of learning outcomes. Although performance-based items and tasks that require problem solving, critical thinking, analysis, and synthesis may be considered superior, especially in measuring more complex, higher-order learning goals, they are also more costly and more time-consuming to create, maintain, and score with high reliability (Robelen, 2009).

Assessments

REFERENCES

American Federation of Teachers, National Council on Measurement in Education, & National Education Association. (1990). *Standards for teacher competence in educational assessment of students.* Washington, DC: National Council on Measurement in Education. Retrieved from http://www.eric.ed.gov/PDFS/ED323186.pdf

Bloom, B. S. (1967, December). Toward a theory of testing which includes measurement-evaluation-assessment (Occasional Paper No. 9). From M. C. Wittrock (Chair), *Proceedings From the Symposium on Problems in the Evaluation of Instruction.* Los Angeles, CA: Center for the Study of Evaluation of Instructional Programs, University of California, Los Angeles. Retrieved from http://www.eric.ed.gov/PDFS/ED036878.pdf

Bloom, B. S. (1970). Toward a theory of testing which includes measurement-evaluation-assessment. In M. C. Wittrock & D. E. Wiley (Eds.), *The evaluation of instruction.* New York, NY: Holt, Rinehart & Winston.

Nitko, A. J., & Brookhart, S. M. (2010). *Educational assessment of students* (6th ed.). Upper Saddle River, NJ: Merrill/PrenticeHall.

Popham, W. J. (2011). *Classroom assessment: What teachers need to know* (6th ed.). Upper Saddle River, NJ: Pearson Education.

Robelen, E. W. (2009, October 6). Budget woes putting squeeze on state testing, GAO reports. *Education Week.* Retrieved from http://www.edweek.org/ew/articles/2009/10/06/07gao_ep.h29.html

Russell, M. K., & Airasian, P. W. (2011). *Classroom assessment: Concepts and applications* (7th ed.). New York, NY: McGraw-Hill.

Stiggins, R. J., & Chappuis, J. (2011). *An introduction to student-involved assessment for learning* (6th ed.). Upper Saddle River, NJ: Pearson Education.

6

What Is *Formative* Assessment?

A s was true with regard to the idea of standards, many educators also believe that *formative* assessment is a relatively new concept in education. Indeed, in recent years increasing numbers of educators have discovered the powerful influence of formative assessment on student learning (Andrade & Cizek, 2010; McMillan, 2007). But formative assessment has actually been a part of education for decades as well.

The term formative was initially introduced in 1967 by Michael Scriven in the context of program evaluation (Scriven, 1967). Scriven defined formative evaluation as, "typically conducted *during* the development or improvement of a program or product . . . often more than once, *for* the in-house staff of the program *with the intent to improve*" (1991, pp. 168–169, italics in the original). In other words, formative evaluation involves gathering information while a program is being implemented in order to provide program developers with feedback on how things are going. If problems are identified, then steps can be taken immediately to remedy those problems and guarantee better results in the end.

The year following Scriven's introduction of *formative* to evaluators, Benjamin Bloom borrowed the term to describe the brief, diagnostic progress assessments he advocated teachers use in implementing an instructional strategy he labeled "mastery learning" (Bloom, 1968). Similar to Scriven's idea of formative evaluation, formative assessments are administered by teachers at regular intervals during the instructional process to check on students' learning progress. According to Bloom and his colleagues,

> Frequent formative (assessments) pace students' learning and help motivate them to put forth the necessary effort at the proper time. The appropriate use of these (assessments) helps ensure that each set of learning tasks has been thoroughly mastered before subsequent tasks are started. (Bloom, Hastings, & Madaus, 1971, pp. 53–54)

Bloom and his colleagues later described their ideas on formative assessments in greater detail.

> Formative (assessments) are intended to provide feedback to both teachers and students. Each formative (assessment) covers a unit or part of the course. . . . We tend to think of learning units for formative (assessment) as involving about two weeks of learning activity or approximately eight to ten hours of instruction in the class. In the early primary grades the unit may be only about a week of instruction. . . . The major point in formative (assessment) is to maximize the learning time and minimize the testing and corrective time. Typically, a formative (assessment) should take about 20 to 30 minutes. (Bloom, Madaus, & Hastings, 1981, p. 63)

Bloom and his colleagues (Bloom et al., 1981) distinguished formative assessments from the regular, more frequent, but less formal "checks" for understanding that teachers use while teaching a particular lesson. Teachers employ these quick checks intermittently throughout a lesson to determine if students are following the lesson and activities, engaging appropriately, making suitable connections, and grasping important concepts. These checks include techniques such as asking questions to which students respond orally or with clickers, having students raise their hands depending on whether they fully understand or need further explanation, inviting students to share with classmates or check each other's work, and similar interactions.

Formative assessments, on the other hand, involve more formal procedures that teachers use to determine whether or not students have mastered the learning goals from an instructional unit. Although formative assessments often consist of pencil-and-paper instruments, they might also be skill demonstrations, task performances, essays, compositions, lab projects, digital or web-based tools, or any procedure teachers use to gather valid information on students' mastery of unit learning goals.

In recent years, theorists and researchers have broadened the definition of formative assessment to include any means of gathering information on student learning that can be used to provide feedback on learning progress and guide revisions in instructional activities. Some of these modern definitions abandon the distinction Bloom and his colleagues made between formative assessments and the less formal checks for understanding. Black and Wiliam (1998), for example, define formative assessment as, "encompassing all those activities undertaken by teachers, and/or by their students, which provide information to be used as feedback to modify the teaching and learning activities in which they are engaged" (p. 7).

Another more recent change in thinking about formative assessments stems from contemporary theories about how students learn and self-regulated learning (Moss, Girard, & Haniford, 2006; Shepard, 2006). These new theories stress the importance of students as formative decision makers who need regular and descriptive information in order to make productive decisions about their own learning (Brookhart, 2011).

This emphasis on students also provides the basis for student-involved assessment (Stiggins & Chappuis, 2011).

Some experts argue that it is easier to define formative assessments by describing what they are not. Cech (2008), for example, stresses that they are not like the long, year-end, state-administered, standardized, required exams that testing professionals call *summative*. Nor are they like the shorter, middle-of-the-year assessments referred to as *benchmark* or *interim* assessments. Other experts acknowledge, however, that the lack of widespread understanding about the nature of formative assessment makes the term vulnerable to misinterpretation and misuse.

Whether one uses Bloom's original definition or the broader and wider-ranging definition of Black and Wiliam (1998), the purpose of formative assessment remains the same. It is a process, strategy, or device used by teachers and students to gather information on students' learning progress in order to identify learning difficulties and guide improvements in instructional activities and student learning.

REFERENCES

Andrade, H. L., & Cizek, G. J. (Eds.). (2010). *Handbook of formative assessment.* New York, NY: Routledge.

Black, P., & Wiliam, D. (1998). Assessment and classroom learning. *Assessment in Education: Principles, Policy & Practice, 5*(1), 7–74.

Bloom, B. S. (1968). Learning for mastery. *Evaluation Comment* (UCLA-CSIEP), *1*(2), 1–12.

Bloom, B. S., Hastings, J. T., & Madaus, G. F. (1971). *Handbook on formative and summative evaluation of student learning.* New York, NY: McGraw-Hill.

Bloom, B. S., Madaus, G. F., & Hastings, J. T. (1981). *Evaluation to improve learning.* New York, NY: McGraw-Hill.

Brookhart, S. M. (2011). Educational assessment knowledge and skills for teachers. *Educational Measurement: Issues and Practice, 30*(1), 3–12.

Cech, S. (2008, September 17). Test industry split over "formative" assessment. *Education Week, 28*(4), 1.

Assessments

McMillan, J. H. (Ed.). (2007). *Formative classroom assessment: Theory into practice.* New York, NY: Teachers College Press.

Moss, P. A., Girard, B. J., & Haniford, L. C. (2006). Validity in educational assessment. *Review of Research in Education, 30*(1), 109–162.

Scriven, M. S. (1967). The methodology of evaluation. In R. W. Tyler, R. M. Gagne, & M. Scriven (Eds.), *Perspectives of curriculum evaluation* (American Educational Research Association Monograph Series on Curriculum Evaluation. No. 1; pp. 39–83). Chicago, IL: Rand McNally.

Scriven, M. S. (1991). *Evaluation thesaurus* (4th ed.). Newbury Park, CA: Sage.

Shepard, L. A. (2006). Classroom assessment. In R. L. Brennan (Ed.), *Educational measurement* (4th ed., pp. 623–646). Westport, CT: Praeger.

Stiggins, R. J., & Chappuis, J. (2011). *An introduction to student-involved assessment for learning* (6th ed.). Upper Saddle River, NJ: Pearson Education.

Assessments

7

Why Are Formative Assessments Important?

Educators have always used different types of assessments to evaluate student learning. For most teachers, assessments provided the evidence they need to determine students' competence and assign grades. For students, assessments usually marked the end of instructional units, the end of the time they need to spend working on that unit's content, and their one and often only chance to demonstrate what they learned.

The idea of using assessments not only to evaluate but also to facilitate student learning dates back to the writings of early educators such as Comenius, Pestalozzi, and Herbart (Bloom, 1974). Still, it was the work of Benjamin Bloom (1968, 1971) that brought this idea to prominence in modern times. Bloom saw value in teachers' customary practice of assessing student learning at the end of each instructional unit. He believed, however, that most classroom assessments did little more than verify for which students the teachers' initial instruction was and was not appropriate.

A far better approach, according to Bloom, would be for teachers to use their classroom assessments as *learning tools*, both to provide students with *feedback* on their learning progress and to guide the *correction* of learning errors. In other words, instead of using assessments only to evaluate students' competence and assign grades, Bloom recommended teachers use them as an integral part of the instructional process to *identify* students' individual learning difficulties and then to *prescribe* remediation procedures. In this way, assessments would not take time away from learning but would serve to assist and enhance learning.

This is precisely what takes place when an excellent tutor works with an individual student. If the student makes an error in answering a question or solving a problem, the tutor first points out the error (feedback) and then follows up with further explanation and clarification (correctives) to ensure the student's understanding. Academically successful students typically initiate their own feedback and correctives. They follow up on the mistakes they make on quizzes and assessments, seeking further information and greater understanding so that they do not repeat their learning errors. Most students, however, need a more structured feedback and corrective process to help them use assessment results to improve their mastery of the concepts and skills.

Benjamin Bloom outlined an instructional strategy to help teachers implement this feedback and corrective procedure in their teaching, labeling it "Learning for Mastery" (Bloom, 1968), and later shortening the name to simply "Mastery Learning" (Bloom, 1971). Teachers who use mastery learning administer diagnostic, *formative* assessments at the end of each instructional unit. But rather than marking the end of the unit, these brief assessments help students identify what they have learned well to that point and what they need to learn better. Teachers then pair specific corrective activities with the formative assessment results for students to use in correcting their learning difficulties. The correctives typically are matched to each item or set of prompts within the assessment so that students need work on only those concepts or skills not yet mastered. In other words, the correctives are *individualized.* They may point out sources of information on a particular concept, such as page numbers in the textbook or workbook where that concept is discussed. They may identify alternative learning resources such as different textbooks, learning kits, alternative materials, DVDs, videos, or online instructional lessons. Or they may simply suggest sources of additional practice, such as study guides, independent or guided practice activities, and shared or collaborative group activities (Guskey, 2008).

With the feedback and corrective information gained from a formative assessment, each student has a detailed prescription of what more needs to be done to master the concepts or skills from the unit. This "just-in-time" correction prevents minor learning difficulties from accumulating and becoming major learning problems. It also gives teachers a practical means to vary and differentiate their instruction in order to better meet students' individual learning needs. As a result, more students learn well, master the important learning goals in each unit, and gain the necessary prerequisites for success in subsequent units.

When students complete their corrective work after a class period or two, Bloom recommended they take a *second* formative assessment. This second, *parallel* assessment covers the same concepts and skills as the first, but includes slightly different problems, questions, or prompts. As such, it serves two important purposes. First, it verifies whether or not the correctives truly helped students overcome their individual learning difficulties. Second, it offers students a second chance at success and, hence, has powerful motivational value (Guskey, 1997).

Bloom also recognized that some students are likely to perform well on the first formative assessment, demonstrating their mastery of the unit concepts and skills. For these students, the teacher's initial instruction was highly appropriate, and they have no need for corrective work. To ensure their continued learning progress, Bloom recommended that teachers provide these students with special "enrichment" or "extension" activities to broaden their learning experiences.

Enrichment activities often are self-selected by students and might involve special projects or reports, academic games, or a variety of complex but engaging problem-solving tasks (Guskey, 2010).

Through this process of regular classroom formative assessments, combined with the correction of individual learning errors, Bloom believed all students could be provided with a more appropriate quality of instruction than is possible under more traditional approaches to teaching. As a result, nearly all might be expected to learn well and truly master the unit concepts or learning goals (Bloom, 1976, 1981). This, in turn, would drastically reduce the variation in students' achievement levels, help lessen or eliminate achievement gaps, and allow many more students to achieve at a high level and experience learning success (Guskey, 2007, 2009). The research confirming Bloom's beliefs is discussed in detail in Chapter 13.

REFERENCES

Bloom, B. S. (1968). Learning for mastery. *Evaluation Comment* (UCLA-CSIEP), *1*(2), 1–12.

Bloom, B. S. (1971). Mastery learning. In J. H. Block (Ed.), *Mastery learning: Theory and practice* (pp. 47–63). New York, NY: Holt, Rinehart & Winston.

Bloom, B. S. (1974). An introduction to mastery learning theory. In J. H. Block (Ed.), *Schools, society and mastery learning.* New York, NY: Holt, Rinehart & Winston.

Bloom, B. S. (1976). *Human characteristics and school learning.* New York, NY: McGraw-Hill.

Bloom, B. S. (1981). *All our children learning: A primer for parents, teachers and other educators.* New York, NY: McGraw-Hill.

Guskey, T. R. (1997). *Implementing mastery learning* (2nd ed.). Belmont, CA: Wadsworth.

Guskey, T. R. (2007). Closing achievement gaps: Revisiting Benjamin S. Bloom's "Learning for Mastery." *Journal of Advanced Academics, 19*(1), 8–31.

Guskey, T. R. (2008). The rest of the story. *Educational Leadership, 65*(4), 28–35.

Guskey, T. R. (2009). Mastery learning. In T. L. Good (Ed.), *21st century education: A reference handbook* (Vol. I, pp. 194–202). Thousand Oaks, CA: Sage.

Guskey, T. R. (2010). Lessons of mastery learning. *Educational Leadership, 68*(2), 52–57.

8

What Are *Common* Formative Assessments?

Increasing numbers of educators today are discovering the advantages of common formative assessments. These assessments have the same purpose, form, and structure as the assessments we described in Chapter 6. What makes them different is that they are collaboratively developed, scored, and analyzed by teams of teachers rather than by an individual teacher (Ainsworth & Viegut, 2006). These teacher teams usually have similar grade-level assignments or teach in the same academic department.

To develop common formative assessments, teacher teams first examine the standards or learning goals for each instructional unit and then collaboratively develop assessments that they believe will capture how well students have mastered those standards or goals. Some teams work directly from curriculum frameworks, guides, or maps, while others use "Tables of Specification" (Guskey, 2005). Team members administer these collaboratively developed formative assessments in their individual classes at about the same time. They then get together to analyze the results and plan corrective activities when needed.

For many teams, the first step in their analysis is to construct a table like the one illustrated in Figure 8.1. This table shows a tally of how many students in each teacher's class answered an item incorrectly or failed to meet a particular performance criterion. These simple tallies reveal several important findings. Specifically:

1. All students answered items 4 and 8 correctly. Generally this is a wonderful result indicating that the standards to which these items or prompts relate were taught so well by all three teachers that all students were able to demonstrate their mastery. It also may be, however, that these items or prompts were structured in way that revealed the correct response or made the correct answer obvious. If inspection confirms that this is true, then the teachers will need to revise these items or prompts on the assessment.

2. Most students in all three teachers' classes did well on items 1, 2, 5, 6, 10, and 11. This shows that the instructional practices the teachers used in teaching these particular standards worked well for nearly all students and should be continued. Only a few students in each teacher's class will need to revisit these standards and continue to work on mastery.

3. Although many students in Jen's class struggled with item 3, most students in Michael's and Chris's classes answered this item correctly. In this case, Michael and Chris might offer Jen advice on how she could revise her instructional strategies for this particular standard or goal.

4. For item 7, most of Jen's students did very well but the majority of students in Michael's and Chris's classes had difficulty. Jen can share how she approached this topic or standard and the strategies she used to engage her students. This could help Michael and Chris develop more effective strategies for teaching this particular

Figure 8.1 Analysis of Items Answered Incorrectly by Students on a Common Formative Assessment

Formative Assessment 3			
Item	*Jen*	*Michael*	*Chris*
1							
2								
3																								
4			
5										
6									
7																																			
8			
9																																	
10										
11							
12																						
13																																																
14																	
15																					

standard. Similarly for item 12, Chris's approach appears to have led to greater success than that of Jen or Michael.

5. Items 13, 14, and 15 address standards that continue to be problems for students in all three teachers' classes, especially the standard associated with item 13. When

this occurs and if the items are found to be appropriate, teachers need to seek solutions outside of their individual experiences and expertise. They might consult an instructional coach, critical friend/coach, district coordinator, teachers in other schools, or other subject area experts. They might explore research evidence on effective instructional practices related to these particular standards or goals. They might consider alternative instructional approaches or activities presented in other materials, teaching guides, or online sources. Because these problems are shared by all three teachers, it's clear they will need to look to resources besides each other to find effective solutions.

The purpose of this kind of analysis is to help all of the teachers involved to improve the quality of their instruction so that all of their students learn well. Of course, teachers need to have the necessary time and resources to conduct these kinds of analyses and to develop instructional alternatives. This means that school leaders need to find creative ways to adjust daily teaching schedules so that teachers can meet to do this important work.

With appropriate guidance, the collaborative preparation of common formative assessments assists teachers in developing better assessment tools. But the most vital aspect of this process is the analysis of results and how teachers use the results to revise their instructional strategies and techniques. Working with colleagues in a supportive environment for the collective benefit of all, teachers can be valuable resources to one another in their improvement efforts. Together they can develop better formative assessments that provide students with higher-quality feedback on their learning. Such collaboration also helps teachers create and implement more varied and more effective instructional alternatives so that more students learn well. Although we know of no high-quality research studies that have investigated the specific benefits of common formative assessments for teachers or their students, we believe the development and use of common formative assessments can provide the foundation from which such improvements can emerge.

REFERENCES

Ainsworth, L., & Viegut, D. (2006). *Common formative assessments: How to connect standards-based instruction and assessment.* Thousand Oaks, CA: Corwin.

Guskey, T. R. (2005). Mapping the road to proficiency. *Educational Leadership, 63*(3), 32–38.

Assessments

9

What Is *Summative* Assessment?

Although applying different forms of assessment to measure different learning goals or standards is nothing new in education, distinguishing assessments on the basis of how results will be used is a relatively recent phenomenon. One of the most frequently cited differences in the use of results is between *formative* and *summative* assessments. Many modern educators accurately relate this distinction to the difference between assessments *for* learning and assessments *of* learning (Stiggins, 2008; also see Chapter 12). But the distinction actually stems from much earlier writing and research on the use of assessment results.

Recall in our description of formative assessment in Chapter 6, we explained how Michael Scriven introduced the terms formative and summative in 1967 in the context of program evaluation. The following year, Benjamin Bloom (1968), and then later with his colleagues Thomas Hastings and George Madaus (1971), borrowed Scriven's terms to describe differences in assessments of student learning.

Bloom, Madaus, and Hastings (1981) defined three features that differentiate formative and summative assessments in education: "The three distinguishing characteristics have to do with *purpose* (expected uses), *portion of the course covered* (time), and *level of generalization* sought by the items in the [assessment] used to collect data" (Bloom et al., 1981, p. 71, italics in the original).

The first and most important distinction relates to *purpose*. Regardless of the format of a formative assessment (e.g., a pencil-and-paper instrument, written composition, skill demonstration, etc.), its primary purpose is to provide feedback to students and teachers on learning progress in order to direct improvements in instruction and guide the correction of any learning problems or errors. In other words, formative assessments are designed *to inform*. As such, they are used at regular intervals *during* the instructional process to diagnose difficulties and then to prescribe specific remediation.

Summative assessments, on the other hand, typically are administered *at the end* of an instructional sequence and provide evidence to certify students' competence and to assign grades or marks. Summative assessments tend to be directed toward a much more general appraisal of learning outcomes. Instead of being used to guide improvements, summative assessments provide teachers with culminating evidence that helps them decide if students have mastered certain content and skills, achieved specific standards, and/or are ready to move on to the next level of learning. Assessments used for accountability purposes also would be considered summative.

Perhaps the best description of the distinction between formative and summative assessments is one offered by Robert Stake: "When the cook tastes the soup, that's formative. When the guests taste the soup, that's summative" (quoted in Scriven, 1991, p. 169).

The second feature that differentiates formative and summative assessments is *coverage*. Again, Bloom and his colleagues (1981) explained:

> [Formative assessments] tend to be given at much more frequent intervals than summative [assessments]. It follows from the purpose described above that

Assessments

formative (assessments) should be utilized whenever the initial instruction on a new skill or concept is completed. Summative [assessment] looks at mastery of several such new skills or concepts. Summative [assessments] are *not* reserved solely for final examinations, although certainly the final examinations given in most colleges and some secondary schools for grading and certification are summative. More frequently, [assessments] of a summative nature are used two or three times within a course to contribute grades toward an overall grade reported to students and parents. (p. 72)

A third feature, *level of generalization*, also distinguishes formative and summative assessments. While formative assessments are designed to measure the concepts and skills presented in a single instructional unit, summative assessments generally tap broad abilities and overall goals from across several instructional units. Summative assessments represent culminating demonstrations of learning. They provide teachers with summary evidence for use in making concluding judgments about the adequacy of students' performance.

To these three distinguishing characteristics, we would add a fourth: *time*. Because of differences in coverage and level of generalization, formative and summative assessments also differ in the time students require to complete them. Formative assessments tend to be more like short quizzes or demonstrations. They are brief checks on learning that students generally can complete in 15 to 25 minutes; that is, about half a class period. Summative assessments, however, more closely resemble large examinations, projects, reports, or exhibits of work. If an examination, students may need an entire class period to complete it. In the case of projects, reports, or exhibits of learning, however, even more extended time for preparation and presentation may be required.

These four distinguishing features are described in Table 9.1.

Table 9.1   Differences Between Formative and Summative
Assessments

Characteristic	Formative	Summative
1. Purpose	Inform students and teachers on learning progress and guide correction of learning errors	Certify the degree to which overall goals have been attained and to assign grades
2. Coverage	Concepts and skills presented in a single unit of instruction	Concepts and skills developed over several units or an entire course
3. Level of Generalization	Specific abilities related to individual instructional unit goals	Broad abilities and overall grade-level or course goals
4. Time	15 to 25 minutes (i.e., half a class period), depending on the content and grade level	50 to 60 minutes or longer (i.e., an entire class period or more), depending on the content and grade level

Assessments

The difference between formative and summative assessments still can sometimes become blurred. This is especially true when teachers attempt to use the same instrument for both formative and summative purposes. Although this may be tempting, Bloom and his colleagues strongly discouraged the practice:

> A teacher might wish to try deriving both kinds of [information] from one [assessment], but there is a danger that such a combination will give the learner a different message from that of a formative [assessment] alone. A formative [assessment] needs to be free

from any overtones of grading so that the student does not come to fear it but instead sees formative [assessments] as an aid to learning. Also, the attempt to combine them would very likely require an [assessment] much longer and more complex than advisable. (Bloom et al., 1981, p. 72)

It is easy to see that both formative and summative assessments play important roles in the teaching and learning process. The distinctions between them, however, especially in terms their purpose and how teachers will use the results, must be kept clear.

REFERENCES

Bloom, B. S. (1968). Learning for mastery. *Evaluation Comment (UCLA-CSIEP), 1*(2), 1–12.

Bloom, B. S., Hastings, J. T., & Madaus, G. F. (1971). *Handbook on formative and summative evaluation of student learning.* New York, NY: McGraw-Hill.

Bloom, B. S., Madaus, G. F., & Hastings, J. T. (1981). *Evaluation to improve learning.* New York, NY: McGraw-Hill.

Scriven, M. S. (1991). *Evaluation thesaurus* (4th ed.). Newbury Park, CA: Sage.

Stiggins, R. J. (2008). *An introduction to student-involved assessment for learning* (5th ed.). Upper Saddle River, NJ: Merrill, Prentice Hall.

10

What Is *High-Stakes* Assessment?

*H*igh-stakes assessments are those to which significant consequences are applied to results. These consequences can be either positive or negative and are generally established through education policy or legislative action at the state, provincial, or national level. Although high-stakes assessments can take on any form—from pencil-and-paper or online instruments to projects, exhibits, or detailed skill demonstrations—they are *always* summative assessments. High-stakes assessments provide the basis for decision making in most education accountability programs.

The consequences attached to high-stakes assessment results may apply to students, teachers, schools, or any combination of the three. Students often must score at or above a prescribed cut-off on a high-stakes assessment to receive course credit, certification, or other benefits. Achieving a high score on the SAT or ACT, for example, can help students gain admission to selective colleges or universities and qualify for certain scholarships. Schools and teachers whose students score well on state or provincial assessments (i.e., score at or above an established level of *proficiency*) often receive special

43

recognition along with increased funding or salary benefits (Guskey, 1994).

The negative consequences attached to high-stakes assessment results, sometimes referred to as *sanctions,* can be quite serious. Students who score below the prescribed cut-off on a high-stakes assessment may fail a course and be denied credit, certification, promotion, or graduation. Schools with significant numbers of students scoring below the "proficient" level on high-stakes state or provincial assessments, or failing to show significant progress, may be denied accreditation. In some cases, they may even face the dismissal of the principal and/or teachers.

The recent push for education accountability has led to a dramatic increase in the number and types of high-stakes assessments that educators must consider. Some high-stakes assessments (e.g., school and college admission tests, and assessments used to grant course credit) have been a part of education for many years and can have significant consequences for students' futures. The consequences for students, teachers, and schools attached to the results from current state and provincial assessments clearly make them *high-stakes* as well. Whether or not these assessments and accompanying accountability programs bring about significant improvement in education will depend largely on how the high-stakes results are put to use.

Well-designed and carefully implemented high-stakes assessments can help focus instructional programs on meaningful learning goals. They ensure greater equity in expectations for student learning across teachers and schools and can unite teachers and students in efforts to perform well. Meaningful rewards sometimes provide the impetus for change. And if results are presented in sufficient detail, they can be used to guide improvement initiatives as well as provide evidence for evaluating the effectiveness of those initiatives.

The downside of high-stakes assessments is they sometimes cause teachers and schools to narrow the curriculum to only those subjects included on the assessment. In some states, for example, this has led to an emphasis on language arts and mathematics and a corresponding neglect of science and social studies. Fearing sanctions, teachers also may spend inordinate instructional time in test-preparation tasks and neglect more engaging learning activities (Boardman & Woodruff, 2004; Jones, 2007). Concern for getting students to score above the prescribed cut-off may cause teachers to neglect students who are far above and far below the cut-off (Booher-Jennings, 2005). In other words, teachers concentrate their efforts on students who are close to making the cut-off score and ignore the learning needs of both gifted students and struggling learners. In addition, making high-stakes decisions about students, teachers, or schools based on a single source of evidence is always questionable (Guskey, 2007; Mason, 2007).

Complicating matters still further is the fact that some high-stakes assessments may not adequately capture student attainment of the specified standards. Polikoff, Porter, and Smithson (2011), for example, examined the alignment between standards and state assessments in 19 states and found that only about half of assessment items addressed state standards. In addition, only half of the standards were included on the assessment. Teachers in these states seemed to be aware of this disconnect. Similarly, McCombs (2005) surveyed teachers and principals about their opinions of state standards and assessments in three states and found that teachers felt that state assessments were *not* good measures of standards attainment.

High-stakes assessments are an integral part of education. In cases where specific levels of competence must be guaranteed, high-stakes assessments are clearly essential. Driver license tests, civil service examinations, and teaching or nursing certification examinations, for example, will always be needed. The success of these assessments as tools in improving educational programs will depend on how results are put to use and the thoughtful application of the consequences attached to those results.

REFERENCES

Boardman, A. G., & Woodruff, A. L. (2004). Teacher change and "high stakes" assessment: What happens to professional development. *Teaching & Teacher Education, 20*(6), 545–557.

Booher-Jennings, J. (2005). Below the bubble: "Educational triage" and the Texas Accountability System. *American Educational Research Journal, 42*(2), 231–268.

Guskey, T. R. (Ed.). (1994). *High stakes performance assessment: Perspectives on Kentucky's educational reform.* Thousand Oaks, CA: Corwin.

Guskey, T. R. (2007). Multiple sources of evidence: An analysis of stakeholders' perceptions of various indicators of student learning. *Educational Measurement: Issues and Practice, 26*(1), 19–27.

Jones, B. (2007). The unintended outcomes of high-stakes testing. *Journal of Applied School Psychology, 23*(2), 65–86.

Mason, E. J. (2007). Measurement issues in high-stakes testing: Validity and reliability. *Journal of Applied School Psychology, 23*(2), 27–46.

McCombs, J. S. (2005). *Progress in implementing standards, assessments, and the highly qualified teacher provisions of NCLB: Perspectives from California, Georgia, and Pennsylvania* (Rand Technical Report No. WR-256-EDU). Santa Monica, CA: RAND. Retrieved from http://www.rand.org/publications/WR/WR256/

Polikoff, M. S., Porter, A. C., & Smithson, J. (2011). How well aligned are state assessments of student achievement with state content standards? *American Educational Research Journal, 48*(4), 965–995.

Assessments

11

What Are *Instructionally Sensitive* and *Instructionally Insensitive* Assessments?

All assessments are designed for a specific purpose. Some assessments measure individuals' competence or level of proficiency in a particular subject area or field. The certification exams taken by teachers, nurses, and cosmetologists, for example, assess the knowledge and skills that well-trained persons in these respective fields should possess. Similarly, most state and provincial assessments measure students' competence or proficiency in specific core subjects.

Having all students attain high scores on a well-designed assessment of competence is a good thing. If the assessment aligns with the learning goals of the instructional program, lots of high scores show that the instructional program achieved its goals. Most students learned well the content and skills they were taught as part of the program.

The extent to which student performance on such an assessment reflects the instruction received is referred to as the assessment's *instructional sensitivity* (Kosecoff & Klein, 1974). While sometimes instructional sensitivity is used to refer to the ability of an assessment to detect differences in the quality of instruction (Popham, 2007), in most instances the term implies both instructional content *and* quality (D'Agostino, Welsh, & Corson, 2007; Haladyna & Roid, 1981; Muthen, Kao, & Burstein, 1991). In other words, an instructionally sensitive assessment should be able to detect differences in the content *and* quality of instruction received by students (Polikoff, 2010).

Other prominent assessments are designed for selection purposes. College admission exams like the ACT or SAT, for example, help colleges and universities decide who to admit. Scores on selection assessments do not reflect a particular level of knowledge or competence, but rather where each student ranks in relation to others. Ranking makes the selection process easier.

Assessments designed for selection purposes try to achieve the greatest possible variation in students' scores. In other words, they must accentuate the differences among students. Having all students attain high scores on such an assessment is *not* a good thing. When students' scores are clustered closely together, discriminating among them becomes difficult, perhaps even impossible. This, in turn, complicates the selection process.

To accomplish these different purposes, assessments of competence and selection assessments include different types of questions or items. Suppose, for example, that a particular concept is recognized as important for students' understanding of a certain subject or academic discipline and, as a result, taught well by nearly all teachers. Suppose too, that because it is taught so well, most students answer correctly a question on the assessment related to that concept. Although this would be a good thing on an assessment of competence, it is not a good thing in a selection assessment. Assessments designed for selection purposes cannot include questions that all or nearly all students answer correctly, regardless of the importance of the concept on which the question is based. Such questions do not discriminate among students and make ranking more difficult.

For this reason, assessments like the ACT or SAT are labeled *instructionally insensitive* (Popham, 2007). If instruction helps most students answer a question correctly, then that question is removed from the assessment, for it no longer serves its purpose. Even if the question asks about a vitally important concept, it no longer differentiates students and is eliminated.

This is why scores on selection assessments tend to be more strongly related to social and economic factors than are scores on competence assessments. Aspects other than those influenced by instruction often account for the differences among students. It is also why it makes little sense to use a selection assessment like the ACT or SAT as a measure of the quality of instructional programs. Why would one use an instructionally insensitive assessment to measure instructional quality? Doing so would be analogous to using a ruler to measure a person's weight. The measuring tool is simply not designed for that purpose.

Having all students take a selection test such as the ACT or SAT may help some realize that they rank high enough to get into a college or university. That would be a good thing, especially for nontraditional students and those who come from disadvantaged backgrounds. But to use the results of an instructionally insensitive selection assessment to assess the quality of instructional programs is highly inappropriate and indefensible. No knowledgeable assessment expert would agree to it—and neither should any legislator or policy maker.

REFERENCES

D'Agostino, J. V., Welsh, M. E., & Corson, N. M. (2007). Instructional sensitivity of a state's standards-based assessment. *Educational Assessment, 12*(1), 1–22.

Haladyna, T. M., & Roid, G. H. (1981). The role of instructional sensitivity in the empirical review of criterion-referenced test items. *Journal of Educational Measurement, 18*(1), 39–53.

Kosecoff, J. B., & Klein, S. P. (1974, April). *Instructional sensitivity statistics appropriate for objectives-based test items.* Paper presented at the annual meeting of the National Council on Measurement in Education, New Orleans, LA.

Muthen, B. O., Kao, C. F., & Burstein, L. (1991). Instructionally sensitive psychometrics: Application of a new IRT-based detection technique to mathematics achievement test items. *Journal of Educational Measurement, 28*(1), 1–22.

Polikoff, M. S. (2010). Instructional sensitivity as a psychometric property of assessments. *Educational Measurement: Issues and Practice, 29*(4), 3–14.

Popham, W. J. (2007). Instructional insensitivity of tests: Accountability's dire drawback. *Phi Delta Kappan, 89*(2), 146–150.

Assessments

12

How Do Assessments *for* Learning Differ From Assessments *of* Learning?

T he origin of the expression, "assessment *for* learning" can be traced back to Peter Mittler (1973), who used it in regard to special education class placement in the early 1970s. Lewis Elton (1982) appears to be the first to link the expression to formative assessment. But by most accounts, assessment *for* learning did not become popularized in general education until the late 1980s and early 1990s.

In an *Educational Leadership* article published in 1989 titled "Assessment for Learning," Michael Martinez and Joseph Lipson described how a new generation of assessments developed by the Educational Testing Service promoted learning by providing immediate and elaborate feedback to students and teachers on learning progress (Martinez & Lipson, 1989). Around that same time Richard Stiggins and his colleagues at the Assessment Training Institute in Portland, Oregon, outlined procedures to make assessments *for* learning by involving students as positive decision makers in the assessment process (Stiggins, 2008). In concert with these efforts, Paul

Black and Dylan Wiliam of the Assessment Reform group in the United Kingdom began reviewing studies of assessment in a wide variety of education contexts and concluded that under certain conditions assessments *for* learning had considerable potential to enhance student attainment (Black & Wiliam, 1998a, 1998b).

The distinction between assessments *for* learning and assessments *of* learning is similar to the distinction between formative and summative assessments. Assessments *for* learning are designed to offer detailed feedback to students and teachers in order to guide instructional improvements and enhance achievement. Assessments *of* learning, on the other hand, are used primarily to document student attainment, certify competence or proficiency, and assign grades. Hence, the major difference between assessments *for* learning and assessments *of* learning relates to their purpose. Most writers consider assessments *for* learning to be any procedure or device that teachers use to gather evidence on student learning for the purpose of providing students with feedback on their learning progress in order to guide improvements in learning outcomes.

In recent years, several researchers have extended their definitions of assessments *for* learning, both to clarify their meaning and to enhance effectiveness. Stiggins (2008), for example, continues to stress the importance of actively involving students as decision makers, not only in determining the format of assessments but also in how the results can and should be used. Similarly, Wiliam (2011) emphasizes that understanding the impact of assessment *for* learning requires a broader focus than the feedback intervention itself. In particular, educators must consider the learner's responses to the feedback and the learning environment in which the feedback operates. He advocates a broad definition of assessments *for* learning that focuses on the extent to which instructional decisions are supported by evidence.

Like formative and summative assessments, both assessments *for* learning and assessments *of* learning have important roles in teaching and learning. The distinctions between them can help teachers recognize broader and more purposeful uses of assessment results.

REFERENCES

Black, P., & Wiliam, D. (1998a). Assessment and classroom learning. *Assessment in Education: Principles, Policy & Practice, 5*(1), 7–74.

Black, P., & Wiliam, D. (1998b). Inside the black box: Raising standards through classroom assessment. *Phi Delta Kappan, 80*(2), 139–144.

Elton, L. (1982). Assessment for learning. In D. Bligh (Ed.), *Professionalism and flexibility in learning* (pp. 106–135). Guildford, England: Society for Research into Higher Education.

Martinez, M. E., & Lipson, J. I. (1989). Assessment for learning. *Educational Leadership, 46*(7), 73–75.

Mittler, P. J. (1973). Purposes and principles of assessment. In P. J. Mittler (Ed.), *Assessment for learning in the mentally handicapped.* London, England: Churchill Livingstone.

Stiggins, R. J. (2008). *An introduction to student-involved assessment for learning* (5th ed.). Upper Saddle River, NJ: Merrill, Prentice Hall.

Wiliam, D. (2011). What is assessment for learning? *Studies in Educational Evaluation, 37*(1), 3–14.

Assessments

13

Do Formative Assessments Improve Student Learning?

Among the multitude of methods and strategies available to educators today, it would be difficult to find one more thoroughly investigated than formative assessments. Much of the early research on formative assessments comes from studies of mastery learning, where the idea originated (Bloom, 1968, 1971; Guskey, 1997). But recent research reviews that have considered an even wider array of studies on assessments *for* learning have yielded comparably positive results.

Research on the effect of mastery learning on student achievement comes from all parts of the world. Studies have been conducted in Asia (Kim et al., 1969, 1970; Wu, 1994), Australia (Chan, 1981), Europe (Dyke, 1988; Langeheine, 1992; Mevarech, 1985, 1986; Postlethwaite & Haggarty, 1998; Reezigt & Weide, 1990, 1992; Yildiran, 2006), South America (Cabezon, 1984), and the United States (Anderson, 1994; Block, Efthim, & Burns, 1989; Guskey & Pigott, 1988; Walberg, 1984, 1986). Results consistently show that the careful and systematic application of mastery learning principles and formative assessments leads to significant improvements in student learning. Some researchers even suggest that the superiority

of Japanese students in international comparisons of achievement in mathematics operations and problem solving may be
due largely to the widespread use in Japan of instructional
practices similar to mastery learning (Nakajima, 2006;
Waddington, 1995).

Perhaps most impressive, a comprehensive, meta-analysis
review of the research on mastery learning by C. C. Kulik,
Kulik, and Bangert-Drowns (1990) concluded:

> We recently reviewed meta-analyses in nearly 40 dif-
> ferent areas of educational research (J. A. Kulik &
> Kulik, 1989). Few educational treatments of any sort
> were consistently associated with achievement effects
> as large as those produced by mastery learning. . . . In
> evaluation after evaluation, mastery programs have
> produced impressive gains. (p. 292)

Research evidence also shows the positive effects of mastery learning and accompanying formative assessments often
extend beyond cognitive or achievement outcomes. Mastery
learning strategies have been shown to yield improvements in
students' confidence in learning situations, school attendance
rates, engagement in class activities, attitudes toward learning, and a variety of other affective measures (Block & Burns,
1976; Block et al., 1989; Guskey & Pigott, 1988, Whiting &
Render, 1987; Whiting, Van Burgh, & Render, 1995).

As noted in Chapter 6, in recent years several researchers
have broadened the definition of formative assessment to
include any means of gathering information on student learning in order to provide feedback on learning progress and
guide revisions in instructional activities. Cowie and Bell
(1999), for example, define formative assessment as "the process used by teachers and students to recognize and respond
to student learning in order to enhance that learning, during
the learning" (p. 102). Black and Wiliam (1998a) define formative assessment even more broadly as, "encompassing all
those activities undertaken by teachers, and/or by their students, which provide information to be used as feedback to

Assessments

modify the teaching and learning activities in which they are engaged" (p. 7).

Within the context of this broader and more encompassing definition of formative assessment, research results on the effects of formative assessments on student learning continue to be impressive. In an extensive survey of the research literature, Black and Wiliam (1998a) checked previous reviews, book chapters, and articles in more than 160 journals. They identified about 580 articles and book chapters to study and, from those, considered 250 of these sources sufficiently rigorous to include in their review. Their analysis showed that formative assessments remain one of the most powerful tools that teachers can use to enhance student learning (see also Wiliam & Black, 1998b).

This broader definition of formative assessment has led some researchers to question the validity of inclusive research summaries, however. Bennett (2011), for example, concludes that because the term formative assessment does not yet represent a specific set of artifacts or practices, study results vary widely from one context and student population to the next. Dunn and Mulvenon (2009) agree, stressing that the lack of an agreed-upon definition and dubious methodology in much of the research leaves a limited body of scientifically based empirical evidence to support that formative assessments directly contribute to improved educational outcomes.

A recent rigorous meta-analysis of studies on formative assessments confirms these reservations. Kingston and Nash (2011) reviewed more than 300 studies that appeared to address the effects of formative assessments in Grades K–12 and found the vast majority had severely flawed research designs that yielded uninterpretable results. They identified only 13 studies that provided sufficient information to calculate valid effects, and those effects were less than half the magnitude described in other reviews. Kingston and Nash (2011) conclude that although the effects of formative assessments alone appear positive, they may not be as large as others have claimed, and more high-quality studies are needed.

Despite debates over the magnitude of their impact, most researchers agree that well-designed formative assessments provide students with essential feedback and inform teachers about the quality of their teaching by identifying concepts that students have and have not mastered (Guskey, 2003; Hattie & Timperley, 2007). Most researchers also recognize, however, that *formative assessments alone do little to improve student learning or teaching quality*. What counts is what happens *after* the assessments.

Just as regularly checking your weight or blood pressure does little to improve your health if you do nothing with the information gained, what matters most with formative assessments is how students and teachers use the results. Unfortunately, many educators today overlook this vital aspect of formative assessments. And by missing this essential component, a point stressed by Bloom (1968, 1971) in his descriptions of mastery learning, they fail to produce the most valuable benefits of the formative assessment process (Guskey, 2008).

In their recent review of the literature on formative assessments, Heritage, Kim, Vendlinski, and Herman (2009) stress the crucial importance of corrective action based on the results of formative assessments. According to these researchers, their analysis "provides evidence that teachers are better at drawing reasonable inferences about student levels of understanding from assessment information than they are at deciding the next instructional steps" (p. 24). Similarly, in analyzing teachers' use of interim assessments, Goertz, Olah, and Riggan (2009) conclude: "When well-supported by their districts and schools, teachers used interim assessment data to decide what to re-teach and to whom, but not necessarily to change the ways in which they taught this content" (p. 2).

There seems little doubt that formative assessments offer educators a valuable tool to improve student learning. But to realize the true benefits of such assessment, attention needs to focus on what students and teachers *do* with the assessment results. To close achievement gaps and help all students learn well, educators must provide students with alternative pathways to learning success, engaging students in diverse

Assessments

corrective activities that offer different approaches to learning. More recently, Black and Wiliam (2009) go so far as to suggest that the task of educators is actually to engineer learning opportunities so that learners can become more expert and more responsible in guiding and furthering their own learning. In other words, they believe that the true value of formative assessments will be realized only when educators help students find ways to gain the high-quality feedback offered by various types of assessments on their own.

REFERENCES

Anderson, S. A. (1994). *Synthesis of research on mastery learning.* (ERIC Document Reproduction Service No. ED 382 567)

Bennett, R. E. (2011). Formative assessment: A critical review. *Assessment in Education: Principles, Policy & Practice, 18*(5), 5–25.

Black, P., & Wiliam, D. (1998a). Assessment and classroom learning. *Assessment in Education: Principles, Policy & Practice, 5*(1), 7–74.

Black, P., & Wiliam, D. (1998b). Inside the black box: Raising standards through classroom assessment. *Phi Delta Kappan, 80*(2), 139–144.

Black, P., & Wiliam, D. (2009). Developing the theory of formative assessment. *Educational Assessment, Evaluation and Accountability, 21*(1), 5–31.

Block, J. H., & Burns, R. B. (1976). Mastery learning. In L. Shulman (Ed.), *Review of research in education* (Vol. 4, pp. 3–49). Itasca, IL: Peacock.

Block, J. H., Efthim, H. E., & Burns, R. B. (1989). *Building effective mastery learning schools.* New York, NY: Longman.

Bloom, B. S. (1968). Learning for mastery. *Evaluation Comment* (UCLA-CSIEP), *1*(2), 1–12.

Bloom, B. S. (1971). Mastery learning. In J. H. Block (Ed.), *Mastery learning: Theory and practice* (pp. 47–63). New York, NY: Holt, Rinehart & Winston.

Cabezon, E. (1984). *The effects of marked changes in student achievement patterns on the students, their teachers, and their parents: The Chilean case.* Unpublished doctoral dissertation, University of Chicago, Chicago, IL.

Chan, K. S. (1981). *The interaction of aptitude with mastery versus non-mastery instruction: Effects on reading comprehension of grade three students.* Unpublished doctoral dissertation, University of Western Australia, Perth, Australia.

Cowie, B., & Bell, B. (1999). A model of formative assessment in science education. *Assessment in Education, 6*(1), 102–116.

Dunn, K. E., & Mulvenon, S. W. (2009). A critical review of research on formative assessment: The limited scientific evidence of the impact of formative assessment in education. *Practical Assessment, Research & Evaluation, 14*(7), 1–11. Available online from http://pareonline.net/getvn.asp?v=14&n=7

Dyke, W. E. (1988). *The immediate effect of a mastery learning program on the belief systems of high school teachers.* Paper presented at the annual meeting of the American Educational Research Association, New Orleans, LA.

Goertz, M. E., Olah, L. N., & Riggan, M. (2009). Can interim assessments be used for instructional change? (RB-51). Philadelphia, PA: CPRE Policy Brief, Graduate School of Education, University of Pennsylvania.

Guskey, T. R. (1997). *Implementing mastery learning* (2nd ed.). Belmont, CA: Wadsworth.

Guskey, T. R. (2003). How classroom assessments improve learning. *Educational Leadership, 60*(5), 6–11.

Guskey, T. R. (2008). The rest of the story. *Educational Leadership, 65*(4), 28–35.

Guskey, T. R., & Pigott, T. D. (1988). Research on group-based mastery learning programs: A meta-analysis. *Journal of Educational Research, 81*(4), 197–216.

Hattie, J., & Timperley, H. (2007). The power of feedback. *Review of Educational Research, 77*(1), 81–112.

Heritage, M., Kim, J., Vendlinski, T., & Herman, J. (2009). From evidence to action: A seamless process in formative assessment? *Educational Measurement: Issues and Practice, 28*(3), 24–31.

Kim, H., et al. (1969). *A study of the Bloom strategies for mastery learning.* Seoul, Korea: Korean Institute for Research in the Behavioral Sciences. (in Korean)

Kim, H., et al. (1970). *The mastery learning project in the middle schools.* Seoul, Korea: Korean Institute for Research in the Behavioral Sciences. (in Korean)

Kingston, N., & Nash, B. (2011). Formative assessment: A meta-analysis and a call for research. *Educational Measurement: Issues and Practice, 30*(4), 28–37.

Kulik, C. C., Kulik, J. A., & Bangert-Drowns, R. L. (1990). Effectiveness of mastery learning programs: A meta-analysis. *Review of Educational Research, 60*(2), 265–299.

Kulik, J. A., & Kulik, C. C. (1989). Meta-analysis in education. *International Journal of Educational Research, 13*(2), 221–340.

Langeheine, R. (1992). *State mastery learning: Dynamic models for longitudinal data.* Paper presented at the annual meeting of the American Educational Research Association, San Francisco, CA.

Mevarech, Z. R. (1985). The effects of cooperative mastery learning strategies on mathematical achievement. *Journal of Educational Research, 78*(6), 372–377.

Mevarech, Z. R. (1986). The role of a feedback-corrective procedure in developing mathematics achievement and self-concept in desegregated classrooms. *Studies in Educational Evaluation, 12*(1), 197–203.

Nakajima, A. (2006). A powerful influence on Japanese education. In T. R. Guskey (Ed.), *Benjamin S. Bloom: Portraits of an educator* (pp. 109–111). Lanham, MD: Rowman & Littlefield Education.

Postlethwaite, K., & Haggarty, L. (1998). Towards effective and transferable learning in secondary school: The development of an approach based on mastery learning. *British Educational Research Journal, 24*(3), 333–353.

Reezigt, B. J., & Weide, M. G. (1990). *The effects of group-based mastery learning on language and arithmetic achievement and attitudes in primary education in the Netherlands.* Paper presented at the annual meeting of the American Educational Research Association, Boston, MA.

Reezigt, G. J., & Weide, M. G. (1992). *Mastery learning and instructional effectiveness.* Paper presented at the annual meeting of the American Educational Research Association, San Francisco, CA.

Waddington, T. (1995). *Why mastery matters.* Paper presented at the annual meeting of the American Educational Research Association, San Francisco, CA.

Walberg, H. J. (1984). Improving the productivity of America's schools. *Educational Leadership, 41*(8), 19–27.

Assessments

Walberg, H. J. (1986). Syntheses of research on teaching. In M. C. Wittrock (Ed.), *Handbook of research on teaching* (3rd ed., pp. 214–229). New York, NY: Macmillan.

Whiting, B., & Render, G. F. (1987). Cognitive and affective outcomes of mastery learning. A review of sixteen semesters. *The Clearing House, 60*(6), 276–280.

Whiting, B., Van Burgh, J. W., & Render, G. F. (1995). *Mastery learning in the classroom.* Paper presented at the annual meeting of the American Educational Research Association, San Francisco, CA.

Wiliam, D., & Black, P. (1998). Meanings and consequences: A basis for distinguishing formative and summative functions of assessment? *British Educational Research Journal, 22*(5), 537–548.

Wu, W. Y. (1994). *Mastery learning in Hong Kong: Challenges and prospects.* Paper presented at the annual meeting of the American Educational Research Association, New Orleans, LA.

Yildiran, G. (2006). *Multicultural applications of mastery learning.* Istanbul, Turkey: Faculty of Education, Bogazici University.

Assessments

PART III

Grading

14

What Are Grades?

In education, grades are the symbols, words, or numerals that teachers assign to evidence on student learning to signify different levels of achievement. This evidence might come from assignments, quizzes, assessments, compositions, projects, reports, performances, or any combination thereof. Teachers gather this evidence from students, evaluate its quality, and then assign grades based on the results of their evaluations (Guskey & Bailey, 2001).

Although some educators distinguish between *grades* and *marks* (O'Connor, 2009), most consider these terms synonymous (Brookhart, 2011; Guskey, 2002). They might be letter grades such as *A, B, C, D,* and *F;* symbols such as ✓+, ✓, and ✓–; descriptive words such as *Exemplary, Satisfactory,* and *Needs Improvement;* or numerals such as *4, 3, 2,* and *1.* Teachers often assign grades to students' individual works or demonstrations. Most teachers also record grades on report cards to communicate their summary judgments of students' performance during a marking period or academic term to parents and others.

In earlier times, teachers assigned grades based on students' relative standing among classmates. For each class, teachers would first rank-order students in terms of their performance and then apportioned grades according to each student's ranking. When teachers used letter grades with this approach, also known as *grading on the curve,* a grade of C meant *average* or *in the middle of the class.*

Recognizing the overwhelming negative consequences of these "norm-based" comparisons for both teachers and students (see Dweck, 2000; Guskey, 2000, 2011), most modern educators base the assignment of grades on specific criteria or standards for student learning (Guskey, 2009). In other words, a grade designates what each student has learned and is able to do, and the performance of classmates is irrelevant.

One of the most challenging issues teachers face in assigning grades is determining what quality and quantity of evidence warrants a particular grade, be it an *A, B, C, D,* or *F,* or *4, 3, 2,* or *1.* Although many experts in education offer suggestions on how to do this (see Arter & McTighe, 2001; Brookhart, 2011; Marzano, 2006), no one seems to have come up with a universally acceptable solution. In particular, no specific mathematical procedure for combining scores from various sources of evidence is defensible under all conditions (Guskey, 2002). Neither is any uniform reasoning or logic process. Hence, any recommended procedure at times will be inappropriate at least for some students and perhaps for many.

In essence, grading is an exercise in professional judgment on the part of teachers. And because of the consequences grades can have, those judgments always must be thoughtful and informed. They must be based on careful analysis of the evidence at hand while considering the validity of each source of evidence for each student. This means that teachers must recognize that any particular source of evidence may be a more valid indicator of true learning and achievement for one student than it is for another.

Due to a variety of personal or situational factors, any single source of evidence may be a flawed indicator of an individual student's achievement. Something unusual in a student's life on a particular day, for example, might have an adverse influence on his or her performance. A personal

Grading

experience at home, an unpleasant interaction with a classmate, a tragedy in the family, or similar event might affect how well a student performs on that particular day. For this reason, no single, standardized procedure will yield fair and accurate grades for all students under all conditions.

The best approach in addressing this issue is always to go back to a statement of purpose for the grade (see Chapter 15). In other words, what is a grade or mark to represent? With the stated purpose in mind, teachers can return to the evidence they have and make decisions, perhaps in consultation with other professionals, about what grade or mark best suits that purpose. This approach may frustrate teachers or school leaders who would prefer a standardized algorithm for determining grades that can be uniformly applied to every student in every class in all situations. But if grades are to represent accurately what students have learned and are able to do, then applying a single, inflexible algorithm is rarely adequate or appropriate.

Teachers must always be able to defend the grades or marks they assign. In addition, they must have evidence on student learning to support their decisions. But their defense must be based on their defined purpose for the grade and their confidence in the validity of the evidence they use in making their decision.

REFERENCES

Arter, J. A., & McTighe, J. (2001). *Scoring rubrics in the classroom.* Thousand Oaks, CA: Corwin.

Brookhart, S. M. (2011). *Grading and learning: Practices that support student achievement.* Bloomington, IN: Solution Tree Press.

Dweck, C. S. (2000). *Self-theories: Their role in motivation, personality, and development.* New York, NY: Psychology Press.

Guskey, T. R. (2000). Grading policies that work against standards . . . and how to fix them. *NASSP Bulletin, 84*(620), 20–29.

Guskey, T. R. (2002). Computerized grade-books and the myth of objectivity. *Phi Delta Kappan, 83*(10), 775–780.

Grading

Guskey, T. R. (Ed.). (2009). *Practical solutions for serious problems in standards-based grading.* Thousand Oaks, CA: Corwin.

Guskey, T. R. (2011). Five obstacles to grading reform. *Educational Leadership, 69*(3), 16–21.

Guskey, T. R., & Bailey, J. M. (2001). *Developing grading and reporting systems for student learning.* Thousand Oaks, CA: Corwin.

Marzano, R. J. (2006). *Classroom assessment and grading that work.* Alexandria, VA: Association for Supervision and Curriculum Development.

O'Connor, K. (2009). *How to grade for learning K–12* (3rd ed.). Thousand Oaks, CA: Corwin.

Grading

15

What Is the Purpose of Grading?

The first and most important decision that educators must make in their efforts to improve grading is to define its purpose. All other decisions with regard to grading policies and practices, as well as the structure of report cards, transcripts, and other student records, will be based on this basic definition of purpose. Educators who charge ahead changing policies and practices without carefully articulating the purpose of grading inevitably encounter difficulties. No other decision is more vital or more fundamental to success in grading (Brookhart, 2011).

Deciding the purpose of grading may appear to be a relatively easy task. After all, nearly every teacher has been evaluating students' work and assigning grades since the first day they walked into the classroom. But most educators find the process far more difficult than they ever imagined. Administrators, teachers, parents, others (e.g., colleges and universities, employers, etc.), and even students often want different things, and developing consensus can be difficult. For grades to have meaning, however, all groups must be able to interpret grades in the same way (Seeley, 1994). This can happen only when everyone involved is clear about the purpose of grading and what grades represent.

When researchers ask educators about the purpose of grading, they find that responses generally fall into six broad categories (see Airasian, 2001; Frisbie & Waltman, 1992; Guskey & Bailey, 2001). These categories include:

1. *To communicate information about students' achievement to parents and others.* Grades provide parents and other interested persons (e.g., guardians, families, etc.) with information about their child's achievement and learning progress in school. To some extent, grades also serve to involve parents in the educational process.

2. *To provide information to students for self-evaluation.* Grades offer students information about the level and adequacy of their academic achievement and performance in school. As a feedback device, grades can also redirect students' efforts and ideally lead to improvements in academic performance.

3. *To select, identify, or group students for certain educational paths or programs.* Grades are a primary source of evidence used to select students for special programs. Passing grades are needed to gain credit for courses and to move on to the next school level. High grades typically are required for entry into gifted education programs and honors or advanced classes, while low grades are often the first indicator of learning problems that result in students' placement in special needs programs. Grades recorded on transcripts are also used as a criterion for admission to selective colleges and universities.

4. *To provide incentives for students to learn.* Although many educators debate the idea, extensive evidence shows that grades and other reporting methods are important factors in determining the amount of effort students put forth and how seriously they regard any learning or assessment task (Brookhart, 1993; Cameron & Pierce, 1994, 1996; Chastain, 1990; Guskey & Anderman, 2008; Natriello & Dornbusch, 1984).

Grading

5. *To evaluate the effectiveness of instructional programs.* Comparisons of grades and other reporting evidence frequently are used to judge the value and effectiveness of new programs, curricula, and instructional techniques.

6. *To provide evidence of students' lack of effort or inappropriate responsibility.* Grades and other reporting devices are also used to document unsuitable behaviors on the part of certain students. Some teachers use grades to encourage compliance with established classroom policies while others threaten students with poor grades in order to ensure more acceptable and appropriate behavior.

While all of these purposes may be considered legitimate, educators seldom agree on which purpose is *most* important. When asked to rank order these six purposes in terms of their importance, some portion of educators typically ranks each one of the six purposes as first—even when the group consists of teachers and school leaders from a single school (Guskey, in press).

When educators do not agree on the purpose, they often attempt to create policies for grading that address *all* of these purposes—and usually end up achieving none very well (Austin & McCann, 1992; Brookhart, 1991; Cross & Frary, 1999). The simple truth is that no approach to grading can serve *all* of these purposes well. In fact, some of these purposes are actually counter to others.

Suppose, for example, that the educators in a particular school or school district strive to have all students learn well. Suppose, too, that these educators are highly successful in their efforts and, as a result, nearly all of their students attain high levels of achievement and earn high grades. These very positive results pose no problem if the purpose of grading is to communicate information about students' achievement to parents and others or to provide information to students for the purpose of self-evaluation. The educators from this school or school district can be proud of what they have accomplished and can look forward to sharing those results with parents and students.

This same outcome poses major problems, however, if the purpose of grading is to select students for special educational paths or to evaluate the effectiveness of instructional programs. To use grades for selection or evaluation purposes requires variation in the grades—and the more variation the better! For this purpose it is best to have the grades dispersed across all possible categories in order to maximize the differences among students and programs. How else can appropriate selection take place or one program be judged better than another? But if all students learn well and earn the same high grades or marks, there is no variation. Determining differences under such conditions is impossible. Thus while one purpose is served well, another purpose is clearly not.

Defining the purpose of grading involves deciding: (1) What do grades mean?, (2) What evidence should be considered in determining grades?, (3) Who is the primary audience for the information?, (4) What is the intended goal of that communication?, and (5) How should that information be used? A sample purpose statement might be

---

PURPOSE OF GRADING

The purpose of grading is to describe how well students have achieved specific learning expectations based on evidence gathered from an assignment, assessment, or other demonstration of learning. Grades are intended to inform parents, students, and others about learning successes and to guide improvements when needed.

Defining the purpose of grading by addressing these five key questions is a vital first step in improvement efforts. After these key questions about the purpose are answered, other critical issues related to grading policies and practices become much easier to address and resolve. In addition, the grades assigned become easier to explain and defend because their meaning is clearer.

REFERENCES

Airasian, P. W. (2001). *Classroom assessment: Concepts and applications* (4th ed.). New York, NY: McGraw-Hill.

Austin, S., & McCann, R. (1992). *"Here's another arbitrary grade for your collection": A statewide study of grading policies.* Paper presented at the annual meeting of the American Educational Research Association, San Francisco, CA.

Brookhart, S. M. (1991). Grading practices and validity. *Educational Measurement: Issues and Practice, 10*(1), 35–36.

Brookhart, S. M. (1993). Teachers' grading practices: Meaning and values. *Journal of Educational Measurement, 30*(2), 123–142.

Brookhart, S. M. (2011). Starting the conversation about grading. *Educational Leadership, 69*(3), 10–14.

Cameron, J., & Pierce, W. D. (1994). Reinforcement, reward, and intrinsic motivation: A meta-analysis. *Review of Educational Research, 64*(3), 363–423.

Cameron, J., & Pierce, W. D. (1996). The debate about rewards and intrinsic motivation: Protests and accusations do not alter the results. *Review of Educational Research, 66*(1), 39–51.

Chastain, K. (1990). Characteristics of graded and ungraded compositions. *Modern Language Journal, 74*(1), 10–14.

Cross, L. H., & Frary, R. B. (1999). Hodgepodge grading: Endorsed by students and teachers alike. *Applied Measurement in Education, 12*(1), 53–72.

Frisbie, D. A., & Waltman, K. K. (1992). Developing a personal grading plan. *Educational Measurement: Issues and Practices, 11*(3), 35–42.

Guskey, T. R. (in press). Beyond tradition: Teachers' views of crucial grading and reporting issues. *Journal of Educational Research and Policy Studies.*

Guskey, T. R., & Anderman, E. M. (2008). Students at bat. *Educational Leadership, 66*(3), 8–14.

Guskey, T. R., & Bailey, J. M. (2001). *Developing grading and reporting systems for student learning.* Thousand Oaks, CA: Corwin.

Natriello, G., & Dornbusch, S. M. (1984). *Teacher evaluation standards and student effort.* New York, NY: Longman.

Seeley, M. M. (1994). The mismatch between assessment and grading. *Educational Leadership, 52*(2), 4–6.

Grading

16

Are Grades Essential to Teaching and Learning?

A lthough it surprises many teachers and school leaders to learn this, strong research evidence shows that grading and reporting are *not* essential to the instructional process. Teachers do not need grades or reporting forms to teach well, and students can and do learn many things quite well without grades (Frisbie & Waltman, 1992). For this reason, the primary purpose of grades and grading must be seen as other than to enhance teaching and learning activities (Brookhart, 2011a, 2011b).

While grading may not be essential to teaching or learning, however, regularly *checking* on students' learning progress *is* essential. To facilitate learning, teachers *must* provide students with regular and specific feedback on their learning progress (Hattie & Timperley, 2007). Equally important, that feedback *must* be paired with explicit guidance and direction to students for correcting any identified learning difficulties (Guskey, 2008). But checking is different from grading.

Checking implies finding out well how students are doing, what they have learned well, what problems or difficulties they might be experiencing, and what corrective measures are likely to help remedy those difficulties. The process is primarily a *diagnostic* and *prescriptive* interaction between teachers and students (see Bloom, 1968; Guskey, 1997, 2010). Grading, on the other hand, typically involves teachers judging the adequacy of students' performance at a particular point in time and then assigning a designated rating or score to that level of performance. As such, it is primarily *evaluative* and *descriptive* (Bloom, Madaus, & Hastings, 1981).

When teachers do both checking and grading, they must serve dual roles as both advocate and judge for students—roles that are not necessarily compatible (Bishop, 1992). Ironically, most educators recognize this incompatibility when administrators are called upon to evaluate the performance of teachers (Frase & Streshly, 1994). Principals find it extremely difficult to be both an advocate for teachers and also their evaluator. The same incompatibility is generally overlooked, however, when teachers are required to evaluate the performance of students. Finding a meaningful compromise between these dual roles can be discomforting for many teachers, especially those with a child-centered orientation (Barnes, 1985).

To resolve this discomfort, teachers need to make clear the distinction between the formative and summative aspects of their evaluation tasks. The vast majority of assessing student learning that teachers do while teaching, perhaps as much as 90% or more, should be formative in nature. In other words, teachers must regularly gather information on student learning progress in order to determine what has been learned well and what the next instructional steps should be. They use this information to provide students with targeted feedback on their performance and to guide corrective activities when needed. In many instances, students use the feedback on their own to remedy individual learning problems or difficulties (Guskey & Anderman, 2008). Because the primary reason for offering this feedback is to guide improvements in learning, there is no need for it to be accompanied by a grade. Doing so would lessen its value as an instructional tool and may actually diminish students' motivation to learn (Butler & Nisan, 1986).

Only occasionally during the instructional process must teachers gather information in order to assign a culminating, summative grade to students' performance (Bloom, Hastings, & Madaus, 1971). Rather than facilitating learning, this information is collected to document attainment and to certify competence. It communicates how well students have achieved established learning goals or standards. By keeping the distinction between these formative and summative aspects of assessment in mind, and by using assessments of student learning more purposefully, teachers can emphasize their role as advocates for students while still fulfilling their evaluative grading responsibilities.

REFERENCES

Barnes, S. (1985). A study of classroom pupil evaluation: The missing link in teacher education. *Journal of Teacher Education, 36*(4), 46–49.

Bishop, J. H. (1992). Why U.S. students need incentives to learn. *Educational Leadership, 49*(6), 15–18.

Bloom, B. S. (1968). Learning for mastery. *Evaluation Comment* (UCLA-CSIEP), *1*(2), 1–12.

Bloom, B. S., Hastings, J. T., & Madaus, G. F. (1971). *Handbook on formative and summative evaluation of student learning.* New York, NY: McGraw-Hill.

Bloom, B. S., Madaus, G. F., & Hastings, J. T. (1981). *Evaluation to improve learning.* New York, NY: McGraw-Hill.

Brookhart, S. M. (2011a). *Grading and learning: Practices that support student achievement.* Bloomington, IN: Solution Tree Press.

Brookhart, S. M. (2011b). Starting the conversation about grading. *Educational Leadership, 69*(3), 10–14.

Butler, R., & Nisan, M. (1986). Effects of no feedback, task-related comments, and grades on intrinsic motivation and performance. *Journal of Educational Psychology, 78*(3), 210–216.

Frase, L. E., & Streshly, W. (1994). Lack of accuracy, feedback, and commitment in teacher evaluation. *Journal of Personnel Evaluation in Education, 8*(1), 47–57.

Grading

Frisbie, D. A., & Waltman, K. K. (1992). Developing a personal grading plan. *Educational Measurement: Issues and Practices, 11*(3), 35–42.

Guskey, T. R. (1997). *Implementing mastery learning* (2nd ed.). Belmont, CA: Wadsworth.

Guskey, T. R. (2008). The rest of the story. *Educational Leadership, 65*(4), 28–35.

Guskey, T. R. (2010). Lessons of mastery learning. *Educational Leadership, 68*(2), 52–57.

Guskey, T. R., & Anderman, E. M. (2008). Students at bat. *Educational Leadership, 66*(3), 8–14.

Hattie, J., & Timperley, H. (2007). The power of feedback. *Review of Educational Research, 77*(1), 81–112.

Grading

17

Why Are the First Grades Assigned So Important?

W hen students return to school after the summer break, their perceptions about school and about themselves as learners are mostly uncertain. It's a new year with new teachers, new books, new classes, new schedules, and new friends. All of these novelties come with the hope this year could be different and better than all previous years.

That uncertainty in their perceptions continues only until teachers administer the first quizzes and assessments around the end of the second week of school. When teachers assign grades to those first quizzes or assessments, the grades put students into categories. And getting out of a category is really difficult (Guskey, 2011a).

Students who receive a C on that first math quiz begin to see themselves as C students. Their uncertainty suddenly becomes fixed, and they begin to accept the idea they are likely to earn Cs in math for the rest of the school year.

When the second quiz or assessment occurs, they expect to receive another C. When they do, it reinforces their perception. Similarly, if they receive a failing grade on that first quiz or assessment, they think all ensuing grades will be the same.

But if they succeed on that first quiz or assessment and receive a high grade, that too is their perception of all that might follow. Research evidence further indicates that these student perceptions are pretty accurate (Guskey, 2011b).

For teachers, this means that they must do everything possible to ensure students' success during the first few weeks of the school year or academic term. For school leaders, it means that they must do everything they can to support teachers in this effort. At every level and in every class, teachers must do whatever is necessary to help students experience successful learning during this critical period—and not fake success, but accomplishment of something meaningful and challenging. It should be something that students did not understand or could not do before, but now can. It should be something that makes students feel good about what they have achieved and confident in their abilities as learners.

The key to motivating students rests with that success. Students persist in activities at which they experience success, and they avoid activities at which they are not successful or believe they cannot be successful.

This is the reason truancy and attendance problems rarely occur during the first two weeks of the school year. They begin to occur after the first graded quizzes, papers, or assessments. In students' minds, the grades they receive on these first quizzes and assessments establish their likelihood of future success. And why come to school if there is so little chance of doing well?

Together, teachers and school leaders also must help parents understand the importance of this time and how essential it is for them to be genuinely involved in their children's education during these first few weeks and then continue that involvement throughout the school year. Routines established at home in this critical period profoundly affect the likelihood of students' success.

Daily conversations at home about school activities help children recognize that their parents value success in school. Providing a quiet place for children to work on school assignments and limiting the time they spend watching television or playing computer games further increase the chances for success. Checking with the teacher to ensure children are well prepared and ready to succeed in learning also can help.

Successful learning experiences during these first few weeks of school do not guarantee success for the entire year. But they are a powerful and perhaps essential step in that direction. Teachers, school leaders, and parents alike need to take advantage of this critical time and use it well. It can make all the difference.

REFERENCES

Guskey, T. R. (2011a). Starting the school year right. *The School Administrator, 68*(7), 44.

Guskey, T. R. (2011b). Stability and change in high school grades. *NASSP Bulletin, 95*(2), 85–98.

Grading

18

Do Low Grades Prompt Students to Try Harder?

A lthough educators would prefer that motivation to learn be entirely intrinsic, evidence indicates that grades and other reporting methods affect student motivation and the effort students put forth (Cameron & Pierce, 1996). Studies show that most students view high grades as positive recognition of their success, and some work hard to avoid the consequences of low grades (Haladyna, 1999).

At the same time, no research supports the idea that low grades prompt students to try harder. More often, low grades lead students to withdraw from learning. To protect their self-images, many students regard the low grade as irrelevant or meaningless. Others may blame themselves for the low grade but feel helpless to improve (Selby & Murphy, 1992).

Recognizing the effects of low grades on students, some schools have initiated policies that eliminate the use of failing grades altogether. Instead of assigning a low or failing grade, teachers assign an *I*, or incomplete, with specific and immediate consequences. Students who receive an *I* may be required to attend a special study session *that day* to bring their performance up to an acceptable level—and no excuses are accepted. Some schools hold this session after regular school hours whereas others conduct it during lunchtime or at other times during the regular school day.

Such a policy typically requires additional funding for the necessary support mechanisms, of course. It requires facilities, staffing, and may even mean additional student transportation if sessions are held after school. But in the long run, the investment can save money. Because this regular and ongoing support helps students remedy their learning difficulties before they become major problems, schools tend to spend less time and fewer resources in major remediation efforts later on (see Roderick & Camburn, 1999).

Students must understand that there are consequences to what they do and do not do in school. They must understand that there are specific expectations for their performance and the reasons behind those expectations. But those consequences of their actions do not always have to be reflected in a grade (see Guskey & Anderman, 2008). Policies designed to encourage positive responses from students are always more effective than those intended to punish students for inappropriate actions or preventable poor performance.

Grading

REFERENCES

Cameron, J., & Pierce, W. D. (1996). The debate about rewards and intrinsic motivation: Protests and accusations do not alter the results. *Review of Educational Research, 66*(1), 39–51.

Guskey, T. R., & Anderman, E. M. (2008). Students at bat. *Educational Leadership, 66*(3), 8–14.

Haladyna, T. M. (1999). *A complete guide to student grading.* Boston, MA: Allyn & Bacon.

Roderick, M., & Camburn, E. (1999). Risk and recovery from course failure in the early years of high school. *American Educational Research Journal, 36*(2), 303–343.

Selby, D., & Murphy, S. (1992). Graded or degraded: Perceptions of letter-grading for mainstreamed learning-disabled students. *British Columbia Journal of Special Education, 16*(1), 92–104.

19

Why Is Setting Percentage Cut-Offs for Grades an Arbitrary Process?

How to set appropriate cut-offs for grades on assessments and demonstrations of student performance is widely debated in education today. Typically these debates focus on what percentage of items students should be expected to answer correctly in order to have their performance judged *proficient* or to receive a grade of *A, B,* or *C,* and so on?

Both policy makers and teachers generally assume that higher percentage cut-offs mean more rigorous standards and higher expectations for student performance. Making the cut-off 80% correct for proficiency, for instance, is considered more rigorous than a 70% correct cut-off. Similarly, the teacher who sets 95% correct as the cut-off for a grade of *A* is considered to be more demanding and to have higher standards than the teacher who uses a cut-off of only 90% or 92% correct for the *A.* This reasoning leads to the belief that raising the percentage cut-off is one way to raise the standards and expectations we set for student performance.

Unfortunately, it's not quite that simple. Setting percentage cut-offs on assessments for grades is an arbitrary decision that says little about the standards or the expectations set for students' learning. What matters most is the difficulty of the tasks students are asked to perform or the complexity of the questions they are required to answer correctly.

The percentage cut-off representing excellent performance on an extremely challenging task or very difficult set of questions might be quite different from what would be considered excellent on a relatively simple task. The tasks or items designed to measure a particular learning goal can vary widely in intricacy and cognitive complexity.

Suppose, for example, we were interested in assessing students' understanding of United States history and specifically their knowledge of presidents of the United States. We could ask an open-ended, constructed-response question such as:

> 1. Who was the 17th president of the United States?

Although this is a very simple item that requires only recall of basic information, it is an extremely difficult item for most students. Typically less than 10% of high school students are able to answer this item correctly. We might then consider asking the same question in a different format, this time as a multiple-choice, selected-response item. For example:

> 2. Who was the 17th president of the United States?
>
>   A. Abraham Lincoln
>   B. Andrew Johnson
>   C. Ulysses S. Grant
>   D. Millard Fillmore

This remains a fairly difficult item for most students. Because of the multiple-choice format, however, about 30% of

Grading

students are now able to answer correctly. Of course, if all students simply chose an answer at random, the limited-response, multiple-choice format would allow approximately 25% of students to select the correct response.

Suppose we next adjust the possible responses, making the distinctions a bit more obvious:

3. Who was the 17th president of the United States?

   A. George Washington
   B. Andrew Johnson
   C. Ronald Reagan
   D. Barack Obama

Now identifying the correct response is much easier and about 60% of students are able to answer correctly. We probably could assume that those students who still are unable to identify the correct response have very limited knowledge of United States' presidents.

Of course, we could make a final adjustment to the possible responses in order to make the item easier still:

4. Who was the 17th president of the United States?

   A. The War of 1812
   B. Andrew Johnson
   C. The Louisiana Purchase
   D. A Crazy Day for Sally

About 90% of students are able to answer this item correctly. Those who do not are usually drawn to the response "A Crazy Day for Sally," perhaps because they recognize it as the one response that does not belong with the others.

Some might argue that knowing who was the 17th president of the United States is a rather trivial learning outcome—and that might be true. The point is that while each of these items assesses the same learning objective, same goal, or same achievement target or standard, each varies greatly in its difficulty.

Suppose that items similar to each of these four types were combined in larger assessments designed to measure students' learning in a high school course. Those four assessments would pose vastly different challenges to students, and the scores students attained on such assessments undoubtedly would reflect those differences. Would it be fair to set the same *proficiency* cut-off or grade percentage cut-offs for each of those four assessments? Obviously not.

Focusing on only a percentage cut-off is seductive but very misleading because tests and assessments vary widely in how they are designed. Some assessments include items so challenging that students who answer a low percentage of items correctly still do very well.

Take the Graduate Record Examinations (GRE), for example, a series of tests used to determine admission to many graduate school programs. Individuals who answer only 50% of the questions correctly on the GRE Physics test perform better than more than 70% of those who take the test—already a highly self-selected group. For the GRE Mathematics test, 50% correct would outperform approximately 60% of the individuals who take the test. And among those who take the GRE Literature test, only about half get 50% correct (Gitomer & Perlman, 1999). In most classrooms, of course, students who answer only 50% correct on an assessment receive a failing grade.

Should we conclude from this information that the majority of prospective graduate students in physics, mathematics, and literature are a bunch of failures? Of course not. Without careful examination of the questions or tasks students are asked to address, percentage cut-offs are just not that meaningful.

Researchers suggest that an appropriate approach to setting cut-offs must combine teachers' judgments of the importance of concepts addressed and consideration of the cognitive

Grading

processing skills required by the items or tasks (Nitko & Niemierko, 1993). Using this type of cut-off or grade assignment procedure shifts teachers' thinking so that grades on classroom assessments and other demonstrations of learning reflect the quality of student thinking instead of simply the number of points students attain. It incorporates the value teachers place on successful performance and teachers' perceptions of the level of thinking that students must use to answer a question or perform a task.

Sadly, this ideal is seldom realized. Rarely does such thought and consideration go into setting the cut-offs for students' performance or the grades they receive. Even in high-stakes assessment situations where the consequences for students can be quite serious, this level of deliberative judgment is not always prevalent.

Making matters even more complicated is the fact that the challenge or difficulty of assessment items or tasks is also directly related to the quality of the teaching. Students who are taught well and provided ample opportunities to practice and demonstrate what they have learned are likely to find well-aligned assessment questions or performance tasks much easier than students who are taught poorly and given few practice opportunities. Hence, a 90% cut-off on an assessment or task might be relatively easy to meet for students who are taught well, while a 70% cut-off might prove exceptionally difficult for those students who experience poor-quality teaching.

Setting grade cut-offs is a much more complex process than most people think and typically much more arbitrary than most imagine. Even when complex statistical formulae are used in setting cut-offs, their mathematical precision is not a substitute for sound professional judgment (Guskey, 2001).

Raising standards or increasing expectations for students' learning is not accomplished simply by raising the percentage cut-offs for performance levels or different grade categories. It requires thoughtful examination of the tasks students are asked to complete and the questions they are asked to answer in order to demonstrate their learning. It also might involve consideration of the quality of the teaching students experienced prior to the assessment. Only when such judgment becomes a regular part of the grading process will we make accurate and valid decisions about the quality of students' performance and ensure the accuracy of grades.

REFERENCES

Gitomer, D. H., & Perlman, M. A. (1999). Are teacher licensing tests too easy? Are standards too low? *ETS Developments, 45*(1), 4–5.

Guskey, T. R. (2001). High percentages are not the same as high standards. *Phi Delta Kappan, 82*(7), 534–536.

Nitko, A. J., & Niemierko, B. (1993). *Qualitative letter grade standards for teacher-made summative classroom assessments.* Paper presented at the annual meeting of the American Educational Research Association, Atlanta, GA.

Grading

20

What Is Wrong With Grading *on the Curve*?

Most teachers and parents grew up in classrooms where they were graded *on the curve;* that is, their performance was judged against that of their classmates or peers. When teachers grade on the curve, a grade of C does not mean you've reached Step 3 in a five-step process to mastery or proficiency. As we described in Chapter 14, it means *average* or *in the middle of the class.* Similarly, a high grade does not necessarily represent excellent learning. It simply means that you did better than most of your classmates. Because so many teachers and parents experienced these norm-based grading procedures as children and believe they understand them, they see little reason to change.

But there are several problems with this approach. First, grades based on students' relative standing among classmates or on the curve tell us nothing about how well students have learned. In such a system, all students might have performed miserably, but some simply performed less miserably than others.

Second, basing grades on students' standing among classmates makes learning highly competitive. Students must compete with one another for the few scarce rewards (high grades) to be awarded by teachers. Doing well does not mean learning excellently; it means outdoing your classmates. Such competition damages relationships in school (Dweck, 2000; Krumboltz & Yeh, 1996). Students are discouraged from cooperating or helping one another because doing so might hurt the helper's chance at success. Similarly, teachers may refrain from helping individual students because other students might construe this as showing favoritism and biasing the competition (Gray, 1993).

A third and perhaps the most serious problem with grading on the curve relates to the assumption that grade distributions should resemble a normal, bell-shaped curve. A true understanding of normal curve distributions, however, shows the error in this kind of reasoning.

The normal bell-shaped curve describes the distribution of randomly occurring events *when nothing intervenes.* If we conducted an experiment on crop yield in agriculture, for example, we would expect the results to resemble a normal curve. A few fertile fields would produce a high yield; a few infertile fields would produce a low yield; and most would produce an average yield, clustering around the center of the distribution.

But if we intervene in that process—say we add a fertilizer—we would hope to attain a very different distribution of results. Specifically, we would hope to have all fields, or nearly all, produce a high yield. The ideal result would be for all fields to move to the high end of the distribution. In fact, if the distribution of crop yield after our intervention still resembled a normal bell-shaped curve, that would show that our intervention had failed because it made no difference.

Teaching is a similar intervention. It's a purposeful and intentional act. We engage in teaching to attain a specific result—that is, to have all students, or nearly all, learn well the things we set out to teach. And just like adding a fertilizer, if the distribution of student learning after teaching resembles a normal bell-shaped curve, that, too, shows the degree to which our intervention failed. It made no difference.

Some individuals defend grading on the curve by arguing that if scores on intelligence tests tend to resemble a normal bell-shaped curve—and intelligence is clearly related to achievement—then grade distributions should be similar. But research has shown that the seemingly direct relationship

Grading

between aptitude or intelligence and school achievement depends on instructional conditions, *not* a normal distribution curve (Hanushek, 2004; Hershberg, 2005). When the instructional quality is high and well matched to students' learning needs, the magnitude of the relationship between aptitude/intelligence and school achievement diminishes drastically and approaches zero (Bloom, 1976; Bloom, Madaus, & Hastings, 1981).

Grades should always be based on clearly specified learning criteria or well-articulated standards for student learning; never on the curve. Those criteria and standards should be rigorous, challenging, and transparent. Curriculum leaders who are working to align grading policies and practices with the standards for student learning and authentic assessments move us in that direction. Grades based on specific learning criteria or standards for student learning have direct meaning. They communicate what students have learned and are able to do, regardless of the performance of their classmates or peers (Guskey, 2011).

REFERENCES

Bloom, B. S. (1976). *Human characteristics and school learning.* New York, NY: McGraw-Hill.

Bloom, B. S., Madaus, G. F., & Hastings, J. T. (1981). *Evaluation to improve learning.* New York, NY: McGraw-Hill.

Dweck, C. S. (2000). *Self-theories: Their role in motivation, personality, and development.* New York, NY: Psychology Press.

Gray, K. (1993). Why we will lose: Taylorism in America's high schools. *Phi Delta Kappan, 74*(5), 370–374.

Guskey, T. R. (2011). Five obstacles to grading reform. *Educational Leadership, 69*(3), 16–21.

Hanushek, E. A. (2004). *Some simple analytics of school quality* (Working paper 10229). Cambridge, MA: National Bureau of Economic Quality.

Hershberg, T. (2005). Value-added assessment and systemic reform: A response to the challenge of human capital development. *Phi Delta Kappan, 87*(4), 276–283.

Krumboltz, J. D., & Yeh, C. J. (1996). Competitive grading sabotages good teaching. *Phi Delta Kappan, 78*(4), 324–326.

Grading

PART IV

Reporting

21

What Criteria Do Teachers Use in Assigning Grades?

As we discussed in Chapter 19, the grades assigned to students' work or performances should always be based on learning criteria, not *on the curve*. In other words, grades should reflect what students have learned and are able to do, not their relative standing among classmates. Most teachers today agree on the importance of this basic tenet of grading. Seldom do they agree, however, on the specific criteria that are most important and what evidence best reflects those criteria. Complicating matters even more is that teachers frequently combine all of these diverse sources of evidence into a single grade to represent students' learning in a subject area or course.

If someone proposed combining measures of height, weight, diet, and exercise into a single number or mark to represent a person's physical condition, we would consider it laughable. How could the combination of such diverse measures yield anything meaningful? Yet every day, teachers combine aspects of students' achievement, attitude, responsibility, effort, and behavior into a single grade that is then recorded on a report card—and no one questions it (Guskey, 2011).

In determining students' grades, teachers typically merge scores from major exams, compositions, quizzes, projects, and reports, along with evidence from homework, punctuality in turning in assignments, class participation, work habits, and effort. Computerized grading programs help teachers apply different weights to each of these categories (Guskey, 2002a) that then are combined in idiosyncratic ways (see McMillan, 2001; McMillan, Myran, & Workman, 2002). The result is a *hodgepodge grade* that is just as confounded and impossible to interpret as a *physical condition* grade that combined height, weight, diet, and exercise would be (Brookhart & Nitko, 2008; Cross & Frary, 1996, 1999).

Recognizing that merging these diverse sources of evidence distorts the meaning of any grade, educators in many parts of the world today assign multiple grades. This idea provides the foundation for standards-based approaches to grading. In particular, educators distinguish product, process, and progress learning criteria (Guskey & Bailey, 2010).

Product criteria are favored by educators who believe that the primary purpose of grading is to communicate summative evaluations of students' achievement and performance (O'Connor, 2009). In other words, they focus on *what* students know and are able to do at a particular point in time. Teachers who use product criteria typically base grades exclusively on summative examination scores; final products (reports, projects, or exhibits); overall assessments; and other culminating demonstrations of learning.

Process criteria are emphasized by educators who believe that product criteria do not provide a complete picture of student learning. From their perspective, grades should reflect not only the final results, but also *how* students got there. Teachers who consider responsibility, effort, or work habits when assigning grades use process criteria. So do teachers who count classroom quizzes, formative assessments, homework, punctuality in turning in assignments, class participation, or attendance.

Progress criteria are used by educators who believe that the most important aspect of grading is how much students gain from their learning experiences. Other names for progress

Reporting

criteria include *learning gain, improvement scoring, value-added learning,* and *educational growth.* Teachers who use progress criteria look at how much improvement students have made over a particular period of time, rather than just where they are at a given moment. As a result, scoring based on progress criteria may be highly individualized among students. Grades might be based, for example, on the number of skills or standards in a learning continuum that students mastered and on the adequacy of that level of progress for each student. Most of the research evidence on progress criteria comes from studies of individualized instruction (Esty & Teppo, 1992) and special education programs (Gersten, Vaughn, & Brengelman, 1996; Jung & Guskey, 2010).

After establishing explicit indicators of product, process, and progress learning criteria, teachers in schools that differentiate among these indicators assign separate grades to each indicator. In this way, they keep grades for responsibility, learning skills, effort, work habits, or learning progress distinct from assessments of achievement and performance (Guskey, 2002b; Stiggins, 2008). The intent is to provide a more accurate and more comprehensive picture of what students have accomplished in school (Guskey, 2006).

Although schools in the United States are just beginning to catch on to the idea of separate grades for product, process, and progress criteria, many Canadian educators have used the practice for years (Bailey & McTighe, 1996). Each marking period, teachers in these schools assign an achievement grade on the basis of the student's performance on projects, assessments, and other demonstrations of learning. Often expressed as a letter grade or percentage (A = advanced, B = proficient, C = basic, D = needs improvement, and F = unsatisfactory), this achievement grade represents the teacher's judgment of the student's level of performance relative to explicit learning goals or standards established for the subject area or course. Computations of grade-point averages and class ranks are based solely on these achievement or *product* grades.

Reporting

In addition, teachers assign separate grades for homework, class participation, punctuality in turning in assignments, effort, learning progress, and the like. Because these factors generally relate to specific student behaviors, most teachers record numerical marks for each (4 = consistently; 3 = usually; 2 = sometimes; and 1 = rarely). To clarify a mark's meaning, teachers typically identify specific behavioral indicators for each performance level. For example, the indicators for a homework mark might be:

4 = All homework assignments are completed and turned in on time.

3 = One or two homework assignments are missing or incomplete.

2 = Three to five homework assignments are missing or incomplete.

1 = Numerous homework assignments are missing or incomplete.

Teachers sometimes think that reporting multiple grades will increase their grading workload. But those teachers who use the procedure claim that it actually makes grading easier and less work (Guskey, Swan, & Jung, 2011). Teachers gather the same evidence on student learning that they did before, but they no longer worry about how to weight or combine that evidence in calculating an overall grade. As a result, they avoid irresolvable arguments about the appropriateness or fairness of different weighting strategies.

Reporting separate grades for product, process, and progress criteria also makes grading more meaningful. Grades for academic achievement reflect precisely that—academic achievement—and not some confusing amalgamation that is impossible to interpret and that rarely presents a true picture of students' proficiency (Guskey, 2002b). Teachers also indicate that students take process elements such as homework more seriously when it's reported separately. Parents favor

Reporting

the practice because it provides a more comprehensive profile of their child's performance in school (Guskey et al., 2011).

The key to success in reporting multiple grades, however, rests in the clear specification of indicators related to product, process, and progress criteria. Teachers must be able to describe how they plan to evaluate students' achievement, attitude, effort, behavior, and progress. Then they must clearly communicate these criteria to students, parents, and others.

Developing meaningful, reasonable, and equitable grading policies and practices will continue to challenge educators. The challenge remains all the more daunting, however, if we continue to use reporting forms that require teachers to combine so many diverse sources of evidence into a single symbol. Distinguishing specific *product* criteria and reporting an *achievement* grade based on these criteria allow teachers to offer a better and more precise description of students' academic achievement and performance. To the extent that *process* criteria related to homework, class participation, attitude, effort, responsibility, behavior, and other nonacademic factors remain important, they too can be reported, but should be kept separate. Doing so will clarify the meaning of grades and greatly enhance their communicative value.

REFERENCES

Bailey, J. M., & McTighe, J. (1996). Reporting achievement at the secondary level: What and how. In T. R. Guskey (Ed.), *Communicating student learning: 1996 yearbook of the ASCD* (pp. 119–140). Alexandria, VA: ASCD.

Brookhart, S. M., & Nitko, A. J. (2008). *Assessment and grading in classrooms.* Upper Saddle River, NJ: Pearson.

Cross, L. H., & Frary, R. B. (1996). *Hodgepodge grading: Endorsed by students and teachers alike.* Paper presented at the annual meeting of the National Council on Measurement in Education, New York.

Cross, L. H., & Frary, R. B. (1999). Hodgepodge grading: Endorsed by students and teachers alike. *Applied Measurement in Education, 12*(1), 53–72.

Esty, W. W., & Teppo, A. R. (1992). Grade assignment based on progressive improvement. *Mathematics Teacher, 85*(8), 616–618.

Gersten, R., Vaughn, S., & Brengelman, S. U. (1996). Grading and academic feedback for special education students and students with learning difficulties. In T. R. Guskey (Ed.), *Communicating student learning: 1996 yearbook of the ASCD* (pp. 47–57). Alexandria, VA: ASCD.

Guskey, T. R. (2002a). Computerized grade-books and the myth of objectivity. *Phi Delta Kappan, 83*(10), 775–780.

Guskey, T. R. (2002b). *How's my kid doing? A parents' guide to grades, marks, and report cards.* San Francisco, CA: Jossey-Bass.

Guskey, T. R. (2006). Making high school grades meaningful. *Phi Delta Kappan, 87*(9), 670–675.

Guskey, T. R. (2011). Five obstacles to grading reform. *Educational Leadership, 69*(3), 16–21.

Guskey, T. R., & Bailey, J. M. (2010). *Developing standards-based report cards.* Thousand Oaks, CA: Corwin.

Guskey, T. R., Swan, G. M., & Jung, L. A. (2011). *Parents' and teachers' perceptions of standards-based and traditional report cards.* Paper presented at the annual meeting of the American Educational Research Association, New Orleans, LA.

Jung, L. A., & Guskey, T. R. (2010). Grading exceptional learners. *Educational Leadership, 67*(5), 31–35.

McMillan, J. H. (2001). Secondary teachers' classroom assessment and grading practices. *Educational Measurement: Issues and Practice, 20*(1), 20–32.

McMillan, J. H., Myran, S., & Workman, D. (2002). Elementary teachers' classroom assessment and grading practices. *Journal of Educational Research, 95*(4), 203–213.

O'Connor, K. (2009). *How to grade for learning K-12* (3rd ed.). Thousand Oaks, CA: Corwin.

Stiggins, R. J. (2008). Report cards: Assessments *for* learning. In *Student-involved assessment for learning* (5th ed., pp. 267–310). Upper Saddle River, NJ: Merrill/Prentice.

Reporting

22

What Is *Standards-Based* Grading and Reporting?

S *tandards-based* reforms are designed to bring clarity and precision to education improvement efforts. As we described in Chapter 1, *standards* in education represent the goals of teaching and learning. They describe precisely what we want students to know and be able to do as a result of their experiences in school. Standards specify the particular knowledge, skills, abilities, and dispositions that we hope students will gain through interactions with teachers and fellow students in school learning environments (Guskey & Bailey, 2010).

Most standards include two components. First, they describe specific elements of *content.* That is, they represent *what we want students to learn.* Standards identify the particular knowledge students are expected to acquire as a result of their involvement in instructional activities. Second, they describe levels of *performance.* In other words, standards also indicate *what we want students to be able to do* with what they learn. These levels of performance typically relate to specific student behaviors. In some cases they might involve simply knowing particular information, such as mathematics facts or scientific principles. In other instances they might describe higher-level cognitive processes, such as the ability to solve complex problems, conduct and analyze the results from scientific experiments, explain complicated processes, or compose meaningful stories.

Educators have made great strides in recent years in developing standards for student learning. The *Common Core State Standards Initiative* (NGA & CCSSO, 2010) in the United States is an excellent example. Educators also have been working hard to create better and more authentic assessments to measure students' proficiencies based on those standards. The one element that remains unaligned with these advances is the report card—the primary tool used to describe students' learning progress and achievement to parents and others. Student report cards today look much like they looked a century ago, listing a single grade for each subject area or course.

Standards-based grading and reporting are designed to remedy this problem. Instead of offering only a single, overall grade, teachers evaluate students' performance on different standards within a subject area or course, and then report the results separately. So rather than getting one, cumulative grade, students receive multiple grades or marks reflecting their performance on particular standards. Some standards-based reporting forms list specific standards that differ from one marking period to another or from one grade level to the next. Others list broader *strands* or *domains* of standards and then offer narrative descriptions that specify the focus of instruction during a particular marking period or term (Guskey, Swan, & Jung, 2011b).

In language arts, for example, instead of receiving a single, overall grade, students might receive separate marks for (1) Reading, (2) Writing, (3) Listening, (4) Speaking, and (5) Language Skills. In mathematics, individual marks might be assigned to students for their work in (1) Operations and Algebraic Thinking, (2) Number and Operations—Base Ten, (3) Number and Operations—Fractions, (4) Measurement and Data, (5) Geometry, and (6) Mathematical Practices

(CCSSO, 2010). Standards-based reporting also requires teachers to distinguish grades or marks for achievement or *product* criteria from *process* criteria related to homework, class participation, attitude, effort, responsibility, behavior, and other nonacademic factors (see Chapter 20). While these aspects of school performance may remain important, in standards-based reporting they *must* be reported separately.

As educators clarify the learning goals and standards they want students to meet as a result of their educational experiences, the advantages of standards-based grading and reporting become increasingly evident. The grades or marks offered on standards-based reporting forms provide parents and others with specific information regarding students' progress and achievement in relation to established learning goals and standards. They help identify students' learning strengths as well as areas of struggle or difficulty. This helps parents better understand what is expected of their children in school and how to target improvement efforts when needed. Although standards-based reporting makes reporting forms more detailed and a bit more complex, most parents value the richness of the information provided, especially when it is expressed in terms they understand and can use (Guskey, Swan, & Jung, 2011a).

Successfully implementing standards-based grading and reporting demands a close working relationship between teachers, parents, and school and district leaders. To accurately interpret the reporting form, parents need to know precisely what the standards mean in each marking period and at each grade level. Educators also must ensure that parents understand the language and terminology used in describing the standards. Well-organized meetings with parents to explain the standards and how to appropriately interpret the reporting forms are essential in gaining parental acceptance and support (Epstein & Associates, 2009; Guskey, 2002; Guskey & Bailey, 2001).

Reporting

REFERENCES

Epstein, J. L., & Associates. (2009). *School, family, and community part- nerships: Your handbook for action* (3rd ed.). Thousand Oaks, CA: Corwin.

Guskey, T. R. (2002). *How's my kid doing? A parents' guide to grades, marks, and report cards.* San Francisco, CA: Jossey-Bass.

Guskey, T. R., & Bailey, J. M. (2001). *Developing grading and reporting systems for student learning.* Thousand Oaks, CA: Corwin.

Guskey, T. R., & Bailey, J. M. (2010). *Developing standards-based report cards.* Thousand Oaks, CA: Corwin.

Guskey, T. R., Swan, G. M., & Jung, L. A. (2011a). *Parents' and teachers' perceptions of standards-based and traditional report cards.* Paper presented at the annual meeting of the American Educational Research Association, New Orleans, LA.

Guskey, T. R., Swan, G. M., & Jung, L. A. (2011b). Grades that mean something: Kentucky develops standards-based report cards. *Phi Delta Kappan, 93*(2), 52–57.

National Governors Association (NGA) Center for Best Practices, & Council of Chief State School Officers (CCSSO). (2010). *Common core state standards initiative.* Washington, DC: Author. Retrieved from http://www.corestandards.org/assets/CCSSI_ELA%20 Standards.pdf

Reporting

23

Why Do Some Parents Have Concerns About Standards-Based Grading and Reporting?

Occasionally parents express concerns about standards-based grading and standards-based report cards. Many believe that a single letter grade or percentage grade for each subject area or course on the report card is quite adequate, and they see no reason to change. Most parents also understand letter grades, or at least believe that they do, because letter grades were used when they were in school (see Guskey, Swan, & Jung, 2011). In addition, since most colleges and universities use letter grades and probably will continue to do so, they want their children to become accustomed to letter grade systems so that they can successfully navigate within such systems when they reach that level.

As part of their improvement efforts, educators need to give special attention to helping these parents understand the problems associated with traditional letter grades and percentage grades, as well as the unique benefits of moving to a standards-based system. In particular, they need to help parents understand that when teachers assign a single letter grade or percentage to students for each subject studied or each course taken, they must combine numerous diverse sources of evidence into that one mark. As we described in Chapter 20, this results in what researchers refer to as a *hodge-podge grade* that includes elements of achievement, attitude, effort, and behavior (Brookhart & Nitko, 2008; Cross & Frary, 1999). Even when teachers clarify the weighting strategies they use to combine these diverse elements and employ computerized grading programs to ensure accuracy in their computations, the final grade remains a confusing amalgamation that is impossible to interpret and rarely presents a true picture of a student's academic proficiency (Guskey, 2002; McMillan, 2001; McMillan, Myran, & Workman, 2002).

Researchers also contend that inclusion of these nonacademic factors in determining students' grades is responsible, at least in part, for the discrepancies frequently noted between students' grades and their performance on large-scale accountability assessments (Brennan, Kim, Wenz-Gross, & Siperstein, 2001, D'Agostino & Welsh, 2007; Guskey, 2006; Welsh & D'Agostino, 2009).

This is not to imply that students' effort, responsibility, participation, punctuality, and other work habits are unimportant. Clearly they are. Teachers at all levels generally recognize the value of offering students, as well as parents, specific feedback on the adequacy of performance in these areas. A standards-based report card allows teachers to do precisely that by reporting on these nonacademic elements *separately*. As such, it provides parents with a clearer and more detailed picture of their child's academic performance in school, along with information on these other, important school-related behaviors.

Furthermore, a standards-based report card breaks down each subject area or course into specific facets or *standards* of learning. The standards within each subject area offer parents a more thorough description of their child's achievement. A single grade of C, for example, might mean a modest level of performance on each of five different learning goals, or excellent

Reporting

performance on three goals but dismal performance on two others. Without the breakdown that standards-based reporting offers, this difference would be obscured. Standards-based grading and reporting provides a more comprehensive picture of students' academic progress by identifying specific areas of strength as well as areas where additional work may be needed. It thus facilitates collaboration between parents and educators in their efforts to help students improve their performance.

As far as preparing students for colleges and universities, clearly the best preparation that any school can offer is to engage students in a rigorous and challenging curriculum, and then do all that is possible to guarantee that students learn excellently what that curriculum includes. A standards-based report card identifies the specific learning goals within the curriculum so that appropriate rigor can be ensured. It also communicates more detailed information about student learning progress with regard to those goals in order to bring about higher levels of success. These special benefits serve to prepare students well, no matter what type of learning environment they enter after they leave school.

Developing meaningful, reasonable, and equitable grading policies and practices will continue to challenge educators. The challenge remains all the more daunting, however, if we continue to use reporting forms that require teachers to combine so many diverse sources of evidence into a single symbol. Distinguishing specific *product* criteria based on standards for student learning, and reporting *achievement* marks based on those standards, allows teachers to offer a better and more precise description of students' academic achievement and performance. To the extent that *process* criteria related to homework, class participation, attitude, effort, cooperation, responsibility, behavior, and other nonacademic factors remain important, they too can be reported, but should be kept separate. Doing so will clarify the meaning of grades and greatly enhance their communicative value.

REFERENCES

Brennan, R. T., Kim, J., Wenz-Gross, M., & Siperstein, G. N. (2001). The relative equitability of high-stakes testing versus teacher-assigned grades: An analysis of the Massachusetts Comprehensive Assessment System (MCAS). *Harvard Educational Review, 71*(2), 173–216.

Brookhart, S. M., & Nitko, A. J. (2008). *Assessment and grading in classrooms.* Upper Saddle River, NJ: Pearson.

Cross, L. H., & Frary, R. B. (1999). Hodgepodge grading: Endorsed by students and teachers alike. *Applied Measurement in Education, 12*(1), 53–72.

D'Agostino, J. V., & Welsh, M. E. (2007). Standards-based progress reports and standards-based assessment score convergence. Paper presented at the annual meeting of the American Educational Research Association, Chicago, IL.

Guskey, T. R. (2002). *How's my kid doing? A parents' guide to grades, marks, and report cards.* San Francisco, CA: Jossey-Bass.

Guskey, T. R. (2006). Making high school grades meaningful. *Phi Delta Kappan, 87*(9), 670–675.

Guskey, T. R., Swan, G. M., & Jung, L. A. (2011). *Parents' and teachers' perceptions of standards-based and traditional report cards.* Paper presented at the annual meeting of the American Educational Research Association, New Orleans, LA.

McMillan, J. H. (2001). Secondary teachers' classroom assessment and grading practices. *Educational Measurement: Issues and Practice, 20*(1), 20–32.

McMillan, J. H., Myran, S., & Workman, D. (2002). Elementary teachers' classroom assessment and grading practices. *Journal of Educational Research, 95*(4), 203–213.

Welsh, M. E., & D'Agostino, J. (2009). Fostering consistency between standards-based grades and large-scale assessment results. In T. R. Guskey (Ed.), *Practical solutions to serious problems in standards-based grading* (pp. 75–104). Thousand Oaks, CA: Corwin.

Reporting

24

If Schools Implement Standards-Based Grading, Will the Grades Assigned to Students Likely Go Up or Down?

In our experience, schools implementing standards-based grading and standards-based report cards generally have seen no difference in the *average* grades of students in particular classes or in the entire school. Nevertheless, it is likely changes will occur in the grades or marks of individual students. Since approximately the same number of students will see improvements in their grades as see declines, when combined these changes average out.

As we described in Chapter 21, some students receive passing grades simply because they are compliant, well behaved, turn in assignments on time, and do whatever the teacher asks, even though they may not demonstrate proficiency on grade-level or course standards. When such non-achievement *process* elements are removed from the *product* or achievement grade and reported separately in a standards-based format, the academic achievement grades assigned to these students are likely to be lower. On the other hand, students who receive low grades because of poor work habits, missing or incomplete homework, or inappropriate behavior, even though their scores on assessments of learning may be high, are likely to receive higher grades.

Similarly, if teachers recognize that grade-level or course standards are unattainable for particular struggling learners and take appropriate steps to modify the standards so that they are more in line with those students' levels of performance and academic history, these students' grades and marks may actually improve. It would be noted, of course, that these grades or marks are based on modified standards (see Chapter 30). Still, it would serve to make the grades a fairer, more accurate, and more honest depiction of students' actual performance in school.

Reporting

25

What Is the Most Important First Step in Implementing Standards-Based Grading?

The challenges involved in implementing standards-based grading can frustrate the most dedicated educators, despite their good intentions. Success requires commitment, thoughtfulness, perseverance, and most important, a systematic plan. The first and most important step in that plan must be to define the purpose of grades, grading, and reporting. Before any revision in policies and practices can be considered or any development work begun, the question of purpose must be addressed.

Although defining the purpose of grades and grading might seem an easy task, rarely is that the case. Even teachers who teach the same subjects at the same grade level in the same school often disagree about the purpose of grading. Some teachers see grading as a matter of discipline and control (Brookhart, 2011a). For these teachers, grades represent the *ultimate weapon* in their battle to ensure students comply with established classroom policies and rules for behavior (Guskey, 2004). Other teachers see grades quite differently. To them, grades are simply a communication tool used to inform students, parents, and others about accomplishments in school and how well students have achieved particular learning goals or standards (Guskey, 2001).

Another challenge in defining the purpose of grades and grading is that different groups often want different things. What teachers view as the purpose of grades may differ from that of students, parents, and even school administrators. For grades and reporting devices to have meaning, however, all groups must be able to interpret them in the same way (Seeley, 1994). This can happen only when everyone is clear about the purpose (Brookhart, 2011b).

Making matters even more complicated are potential differences in purpose of grades assigned to assessments or performance, and those included on report cards or cumulative records. While some educators consider the purpose of these different grades to be the same, others see them as serving quite different purposes.

As we discussed in Chapter 15, in defining the purpose of grades, educators need to decide: (1) what information to communicate, (2) who is the primary audience for that information, and (3) how that information should be used. In terms of individual assignments, assessments, or performances, for example, a typical statement of purpose for grades would be:

> The purpose of this grade is to communicate to students and their parents how well each individual has performed in relation to the learning standards and expectations set for this particular assignment or assessment.

If included in a teacher's grading policy, a purpose statement such as this makes clear why assignments and assessments are graded and what those grades represent.

Reporting

Because report card grades represent cumulative or summary evaluations of students' performance over a series of learning units or tasks, their purpose may be different. For example:

The purpose of the grades included on this report card is to describe each student's learning progress based on our school's learning standards for each grade level or course. These grades are intended to inform parents and guardians about students' learning successes and to guide improvements when needed.

Another example would be:

The purpose of this report card is to communicate with parents and students about the achievement of specific learning goals. It identifies students' levels of progress with regard to those goals, areas of strength, and areas where additional time and effort are needed.

A purpose statement such as this describes what grades mean and provides an indication of what evidence is used in determining grades. It also clarifies that evidence on class behavior, work habits, responsibility, and effort are not included in these grades. If important, these aspects of students' performance are reported elsewhere (see Chapter 20).

Statements of purpose for grades should be included in every teacher's classroom grading policy. The purpose of report card grades or marks should be printed in a special box on the front of the report card for all readers to view before they consider any other information (Guskey & Bailey, 2010). This helps ensure that everyone understands the grades' meaning and intent. It also helps clarify the reasons behind the reporting process and how information included in the report card can and should be used. Although we know of no research evidence that demonstrates one particular purpose to be better, more important, or more acceptable than any other across different contexts, our experience shows that reaching consensus on the purpose of grades and grading is vital to the success of any reform effort.

The process of deciding the purpose of grades, grading, report cards, and transcripts can prove challenging. Serious debates often arise that can significantly forestall reforms. As difficult as this process might be, however, addressing questions about purpose remains a vital first step. Defending the grade assigned to the performance of any student always comes down to its defined purpose. In addition, all of the other crucial decisions regarding reporting format, frequency of reporting, the symbols or marks used, and the like, become much easier when consensus about purpose of grading is reached at the beginning of reform process.

REFERENCES

Brookhart, S. M. (2011a). *Grading and learning: Practices that support student achievement.* Bloomington, IN: Solution Tree Press.

Brookhart, S. M. (2011b). Starting the conversation about grading. *Educational Leadership, 69*(3), 10–14.

Guskey, T. R. (2001). Helping standards make the grade. *Educational Leadership, 59*(1), 20–27.

Guskey, T. R. (2004). Zero alternatives. *Principal Leadership, 5*(2), 49–53.

Guskey, T. R., & Bailey, J. M. (2010). *Developing standards-based report cards.* Thousand Oaks, CA: Corwin.

Seeley, M. M. (1994). The mismatch between assessment and grading. *Educational Leadership, 52*(2), 4–6.

Reporting

26

What Is the Best Way to Inform Parents About Moving to Standards-Based Grading?

Parents and guardians can be some of the strongest advocates for standards-based grading and the use of standards-based report cards. They can also be some of the most adamant opponents. Many parents are comfortable with traditional report cards that offer a single grade for each subject or course. They understand these forms, or believe that they do, because such forms closely resemble the report cards they received when they were in school two or three decades ago. Standards-based grading and report cards challenge parents' comfort with reporting simply because they are different. In addition, some parents fear that changing grading policies and the report card so drastically could be potentially harmful to their child's success in school and beyond.

The parents and guardians of high-achieving students sometimes worry that standards-based grading and reporting will no longer permit their child's exceptional talent to be recognized (Guskey, Swan, & Jung, 2011a). Their concerns stem from the belief that grades should serve to differentiate students on the basis of demonstrated talent. Students who show superior talent receive high grades, whereas those who display lesser talent receive lower grades.

To succeed in reforming grading and reporting, educators must help these parents understand that in a standards-based approach, the focus is not on *differentiating* talent but on *developing* talent (Guskey, 2011). After clarifying precisely what they want students to learn and be able to do, teachers do everything possible to ensure that *all* students learn those things well. If successful in their efforts, there will be little or no variation in measures of student learning. All students attain high scores on measures of achievement that address those standards, and all might receive high grades. Fast learners who quickly demonstrate their proficiency on the standards are provided opportunities to broaden and extend their learning, of course (Guskey, 2010). Although this expanded work should be noted and recognized, it may not be evident in grades that reflect performance on established grade-level or course standards.

The parents and guardians of struggling learners, however, typically have a very different perspective. Many of them find traditional report cards to be meaningless. The low grades their child receives only confirm what they already know: that their child is, indeed, struggling. A single overall grade tells them nothing about the learning goals on which their child's performance was judged, areas that might be unique strengths, or areas of difficulty. In addition, traditional report cards give families no guidance or direction as to how they might help, even if they are highly committed to offering whatever assistance their child might need (Jung & Guskey, 2012).

In our experience, parents and guardians can become powerful allies in implementing standards-based grading policies and report cards if they are made aware of why the change is being made and what advantages such change will bring. Some schools accomplish this early in the implementation process by involving parents and guardians on development teams. In other schools, teachers and building leaders use School Council meetings or Parent Teacher Association (PTA) meetings to explain the rationale behind the development of the new reporting policies and accompanying report cards, share draft versions, answer questions, and request parent input.

One of the most effective approaches we have used in gaining parent involvement and support for standards-based grading is to begin implementation by sending home to families two report cards. The first is the traditional one currently in use. The second is the newly developed standards-based reporting form. Typically we do this for two reporting periods so that families can see students' progress on the standards. We then survey parents and guardians, asking them what they like and do not like about each form, and which form they would prefer receiving. In every instance the overwhelming majority of parents choose the standards-based reporting form (Guskey, Swan, & Jung, 2011b). And because of the detailed information offered in the standards-based form, parents and guardians often become some of the strongest advocates for change.

REFERENCES

Guskey, T. R. (2010). Lessons of mastery learning. *Educational Leadership, 68*(2), 52–57.

Guskey, T. R. (2011). Five obstacles to grading reform. *Educational Leadership, 69*(3), 16–21.

Guskey, T. R., Swan, G. M., & Jung, L. A. (2011a). *Parents' and teachers' perceptions of standards-based and traditional report cards.* Paper presented at the annual meeting of the American Educational Research Association, New Orleans, LA.

Guskey, T. R., Swan, G. M., & Jung, L. A. (2011b). Grades that mean something: Kentucky develops standards-based report cards. *Phi Delta Kappan, 93*(2), 52–57.

Jung, L. A., & Guskey, T. R. (2012). *Grading exceptional and struggling learners.* Thousand Oaks, CA: Corwin.

27

What Is the Best Way to Encourage Parents to Make Comments on the Report Card?

A s we emphasized in previous works (Guskey & Bailey, 2010; Jung & Guskey, 2012), every standards-based report card should be designed to include a section that requests comments from parents or guardians as well as students. This gives families the chance to raise questions and seek additional clarification of any information included in the report card. It also encourages family involvement in learning and shows parents that teachers and school leaders value their input and feedback.

Occasionally, however, teachers find parents are reluctant to offer comments. Report cards are returned with a parent's or guardian's signature but nothing more. In some cases, schools try to resolve this by listing a series of statements or questions about the report card and asking parents or guardians simply to check any that apply. One question nearly all include asks families if they would like to schedule a parent–teacher conference to discuss the report card and/or the child's learning progress. Although helpful, this approach significantly restricts the scope of responses families might provide.

In our experience, two reasons account for families' reluctance to offer more detailed, written comments. The first is parents' and guardians' uncertainty about how their questions or comments will be received by teachers. Questioning a teacher about how a particular grade or mark was determined might be seen as challenging the teacher's judgment or authority. Teachers who feel this way might then be harsher in judging their child's performance in the future, jeopardizing the chances of success.

To waylay this fear, teachers need to stress their openness to parents' and guardians' comments and actively encourage the expression of questions or concerns. Some teachers do this during open house meetings or parent–teacher conferences. Other teachers send personal notes to parents or use follow-up e-mail messages or phone calls after report cards are sent home.

A second reason for the reluctance to make comments relates to parents' and guardians' uncertainty or lack of confidence in their own language or writing abilities. Some parents' educational backgrounds left them with limited skills in written expression. Adding comments on a report card would not only reveal these limitations, it might prove embarrassing to their child—and no parent or guardian wants to do that. Likewise, the families of students who are English learners often feel uncomfortable about their own limited English skills. Even those who may be fairly competent in oral language often struggle with writing.

Teachers need to make special efforts to alleviate such concerns. Open house meetings and parent–teacher conferences provide an excellent opportunity to interact with these parents when they are able to attend. Personal notes, e-mail messages, and phone calls can be useful as well. But in some cases, teachers need to make special efforts to meet with parents or guardians at times that suit the family's schedule or even visit students' homes. Visits to students' homes made before the school year begins can be particularly helpful.

These types of interactions do wonders to break down communication barriers between homes and schools (Epstein and Associates, 2009). They also show parents and guardians that educators sincerely care about their children and are committed to their success in school.

REFERENCES

Epstein, J. L., & Associates. (2009). *School, family, and community partnerships: Your handbook for action* (3rd ed.). Thousand Oaks, CA: Corwin.

Guskey, T. R., & Bailey, J. M. (2010). *Developing standards-based report cards.* Thousand Oaks, CA: Corwin.

Jung, L. A., & Guskey, T. R. (2012). *Grading exceptional and struggling learners.* Thousand Oaks, CA: Corwin.

Reporting

28

Will Standards-Based Grading Improve Student Learning?

O f all the questions we are asked with regard to standards-based grading and reporting, this is undoubtedly the most frequent. It is also the question for which we have the least definitive answer.

Admittedly, at this time we know of no well-designed, systematic studies that have linked the implementation of standards-based grading or standards-based report cards to improvements in student learning. That is to say that to our knowledge, there is neither confirmation that such a link exists nor strong evidence to show that it does not. Although such studies may be forthcoming, we know of none that have yet been conducted and their results reported.

In a larger sense, however, why would we expect changing grading practices or the report card to affect student learning in any way, positive or negative? Changing the way we evaluate and report information on student learning has no direct or immediate effect on how students are taught or what they learn. Any potential impact on curriculum or instruction would be tangential at best. So why would we expect standards-based grading or report cards to influence student learning?

From our perspective, standards-based grading and reporting are more about communicating better and more accurate information to families and students *in order to provide the basis for improving student learning.* Whether or not this leads to specific improvements depends not on the information itself, but on how that information is used (Guskey, 2008).

Another way to think about this issue is to see it as analogous to improving performance in a sporting event. If we were to tell you the score of a game you were playing, would that help you play better? Probably not. Similarly, if we were to tell you that in the game, these are the things you are doing well and these are the things you need to improve, would that alone improve your play? Also probably not. But if we were truly interested in working together to improve your performance, which of these two different types of information is more likely to be helpful? Obviously, it's the latter.

That is exactly what standards-based grading and reporting are designed to do. Instead of offering only a nebulous, overall indicator of performance (i.e., the score of the game), it provides families and students with detailed information on school performance so that improvement efforts can be more targeted and effective. This is relevant for the families of all students, but especially those of struggling learners who want and need specific guidance in their efforts to help their children improve (Jung & Guskey, 2012). So while standards-based grading and reporting alone may not improve student learning, it can be an important, and perhaps necessary factor in the process.

REFERENCES

Guskey, T. R. (2008). The rest of the story. *Educational Leadership,* 65(4), 28–35.

Jung, L. A., & Guskey, T. R. (2012). *Grading exceptional and struggling learners.* Thousand Oaks, CA: Corwin.

Reporting

PART V

Grading and Reporting for Exceptional and Struggling Learners

29

Who Are *Exceptional* and *Struggling* Learners?

The terms *exceptional learner* and *struggling learner* are used to describe several groups of students. In this section, the category of *exceptional or struggling learner* includes students who have specific disabilities, those who are English learners (ELs), and those receiving intensive intervention through a response-to-intervention (RTI) model. Together, these students are estimated to make up approximately 20% of the student population; therefore, it is important for educators at all levels to know the criteria for qualifying for each.

One category of struggling learners includes students for whom English is not their primary language and who have limited skills in reading, writing, speaking, and understanding English. Students classified as English learners make up approximately 10% of the pre-kindergarten through 12th grade population in the United States (Gotlieb, 2006). About two thirds of the EL population is elementary aged (Gotlieb, 2006), and, thus, many are not only developing English skills but are *dual language learners*, still learning the primary language spoken in their homes. ELs often have difficulty across all subject areas until they gain some minimal level of proficiency with the English language. The challenges these students face in language arts can persist for years. Reporting their level of proficiency on subject area standards during the time they are mastering grade-level English language skills poses major challenges for teachers. In addition, understanding the meaning of the grades assigned to ELs can be particularly confusing for their parents, who are likely to have limited English language skills.

A second category of struggling learners is students who have disabilities and qualify for special education services through the Individuals with Disabilities Education Act (2004). We also refer to these students as *exceptional learners*. By fifth grade, nearly 12% of students receive some form of special education services in the United States (Herring, McGrath, & Buckley, 2007). Furthermore, the amount of time students with disabilities spend in general education classes has increased dramatically in recent years (Data Accountability Center, 2010). As a result, nearly every classroom teacher today must face the instructional challenges presented by these students with little guidance or direction from regular education experts.

Although there is a wealth of research indicating the positive effects of including students with disabilities in regular education classrooms (e.g., Baker, Wang, & Walberg, 1995; Carlberg & Kavale, 1980; Hunt, Farron-Davis, Beckstead, Curtis, & Goetz, 1994; Waldron, 1998), the process poses significant difficulties with regard to grading and reporting on the performance of these students. It is little wonder that reporting on the progress of students with disabilities is the Individuals with Disabilities Education Act requirement for individualized education programs (IEPs) that states have the greatest difficulty meeting (Etscheidt, 2006).

The most common category of disability is specific learning disability. Learning disability (LD) is a neurological disorder that causes difficulty with academic performance. Students with LD may have trouble with any number of academic tasks, including reading, writing, organizing information, solving problems, or recalling information. A common misconception is that individuals with learning disabilities have lower than average intelligence. But individuals with learning disabilities often have IQs far above average (Horowitz, 2006). Nearly 2.5 million U.S. students receive special education for learning disability (Data Accountability Center, 2010), meaning most teachers will have several students in every class each year who have this disability.

Some students who qualify for special education have moderate or severe disabilities, and often qualify based on diagnosed medical condition(s). Such students tend to be significantly behind their classmates in several or all subject areas. Completing a traditional report card for students with significant disabilities can be especially problematic for teachers. Most consider it unfair to assign failing grades to students with moderate or severe disabilities who try hard but still are unable to demonstrate proficiency on grade-level standards.

Furthermore, legal provisions require that individualized education programs (IEPs) written for children with disabilities enable them "to achieve passing marks and advance from grade to grade" (*Board of Education v. Rowley*, 1982, p. 203). From a legal perspective, a failing grade may indicate that appropriate educational services were *not* provided. At the same time, assigning passing marks to students who have not yet met grade-level performance standards also seems inappropriate because it inaccurately portrays such students' actual level of achievement. For these reasons the parents of children with moderate to severe disabilities rarely find the report card to be informative or useful (Jung, 2009; Jung & Guskey, 2007, 2010, 2011, 2012).

The final category of struggling learner is students who are struggling enough to require intensive intervention, often within a response-to-intervention (RTI) framework. RTI is a set of assessment and intervention practices that allows teachers to identify early those students who may have individual learning difficulties and then to address those difficulties directly with evidence-based instructional strategies (Mellard & Johnson, 2008). For some students, a short period of intensive intervention remedies the difficulties, and no further special services are needed. For others, long-term intensive intervention is needed to maintain sufficient progress.

As with the other categories of struggling learners, teachers may feel confused about how to assign grades to a student who is receiving intensive intervention. Although the student may not be meeting grade-level standards, most teachers may find it difficult to assign a failing grade to a student who is putting forth extraordinary effort and making progress.

REFERENCES

Baker, E. T., Wang, M. C., & Walberg, H. J. (1995). The effects of inclusion on learning. *Educational Leadership, 52*(4), 33–35.

Board of Education v. Rowley, 458 U.S. 176 (1982).

Carlberg, C., & Kavale, K. A. (1980). The efficacy of special versus regular class placement for exceptional children: A meta-analysis. *Journal of Special Education, 14,* 296–309.

Data Accountability Center. (June, 2010). *Part B Child Count, 2008.* Retrieved June 23, 2012, from http://www.ideadata.org/PartBChildCount.asp

Etscheidt, S. K. (2006). Progress monitoring: Legal issues and recommendations for IEP teams. *Teaching Exceptional Children, 38*(3), 56–60.

Gotlieb, M. (2006). *Assessing English language learners: Bridges from language proficiency to academic achievement.* Thousand Oaks, CA: Corwin.

Herring, W. L., McGrath, D. J., & Buckley. J. A. (2007). *Demographic and school characteristics of students receiving special education in the elementary grades (Issue Brief. NCES 2007–005).* Washington, DC: National Center for Education Statistics, U.S. Department of Education.

Horowitz, S. H. (2006). *Checking up on learning disabilities. National Center for Learning Disabilities.* Retrieved from http://www.ncld.org/ld-basics/ld-explained/basic-facts/checking-up-on-learning-disabilities

Hunt, P., Farron-Davis, F., Beckstead, S., Curtis, D., & Goetz, L. (1994). Evaluating the effects of placement of students with

Struggling Learners

severe disabilities in general education versus special classes. *Journal of the Association for Persons with Severe Handicaps, 19,* 200–214.

Individuals with Disabilities Education Improvement Act, 20 U.S.C. § 1400 to 1482 (2004).

Jung, L. A. (2009). The challenges of grading and reporting in special education: An inclusive grading model (pp. 27–40). In T. R. Guskey (Ed.), *Practical solutions for serious problems in standards-based grading.* Thousand Oaks, CA: Corwin.

Jung, L. A., & Guskey, T. R. (2007). Standards-based grading and reporting: A model for special education. *Teaching Exceptional Children, 40*(2), 48–53.

Jung, L. A., & Guskey, T. R. (2010). Grading exceptional learners. *Educational Leadership, 67*(5), 31–35.

Jung, L. A., & Guskey, T. R. (2011). Fair and accurate grading for exceptional learners. *Principal Leadership, 12*(3), 32–37.

Jung, L. A., & Guskey, T. R. (2012). *Grading exceptional and struggling learners.* Thousand Oaks, CA: Corwin.

Mellard, D. F., & Johnson, E. (2008). *RTI: A practitioner's guide to implementing response to intervention.* Thousand Oaks, CA: Corwin.

Waldron, N. L. (1998). The effects of an inclusive school program on students with mild and severe learning disabilities. *Exceptional Children, 64,* 395–405.

30

How Do We Assign Grades to Exceptional and Struggling Learners Who Require Modifications?

Every teacher is faced with the challenge of how to assign grades to exceptional and struggling learners. But few teachers receive any guidance on how they should approach this task. As a result, they arrive at the end of the grading period questioning how to assign meaningful, fair, and legal grades for such students. Lacking explicit recommendations, most general education teachers make individual, informal grading adaptations for struggling learners (Polloway et al., 1994). The adaptations generally fall into five categories:

1. grading on individualized goals;

2. grading based on improvement over past performance;

3. weighting assignments differently;

4. including indicators of effort or behavior in the grade; and

5. modifying the grading scale (Silva, Munk, & Bursuck, 2005).

Each of the above grading adaptations almost always results in higher report card grades for the student. Unfortunately, a higher grade is the only positive outcome of adapting grades in these ways. These new grades are not necessarily accurate nor do they offer better information about a student's true academic performance. Because individual grading adaptations change the ruler by which students' performance is measured, understanding the meaning of adapted grades is impossible. Does an *A* mean that the student met criteria? Or does it mean the student demonstrated high effort? Maybe the *A* means the student participated well.

A primary reason that teachers adapt grades is they believe adjustments that make higher grades attainable will encourage struggling learners to try even harder (Silva et al., 2005). In addition, these adaptations provide students who are unable to meet grade-level standards with the opportunity to earn higher grades, which seems only fair. But in reality, these adapted grades can lead such students to believe that their grades are result of who they are, not what they do. This, in turn, leads to decreased student motivation (Ring & Reetz, 2000). Grading adaptations also introduce issues of injustice to other students who, along with many of their teachers, feel that adapted grades are inappropriate and unfair (Bursuck, Munk, & Olson, 1999). Furthermore, even with these adaptations, most struggling learners continue to receive low passing grades, placing them at high risk for low self-esteem and for dropping out of school (Donahue & Zigmond, 1990).

Instead of asking "How should I measure . . . ?" at the end of the marking period, a far better approach is for teachers to ask, "What should I measure?" at the beginning of the marking period. In other words, teams of educators working collaboratively should decide up front what are the most appropriate expectations for each student. Once these expectations have been identified, measuring students' performance in relation to those standards can be clear, consistent, and equitable. This approach provides the basis for our Inclusive Grading Model shown in Figure 30.1. For extended reading on grading exceptional learners, see Jung (2009) and

Jung and Guskey (2007, 2010, 2012). The model's five steps include the following:

1. Determine if adaptations are needed.

2. Determine if an accommodation or a modification is needed.

3. Establish the appropriate criteria for each area requiring modification.

4. Grade based on the modified standard.

5. Communicate the meaning of the grade.

STEP 1. DETERMINE WHETHER ADAPTATIONS ARE NEEDED

The first step is to determine if each major grade-level expectation is appropriate for the student. To guide this discussion, teams should ask the general education teachers to consider the most critical skills students are expected to master at this grade level. The key question is, "Can we can expect the student to achieve this expectation without special support?" If the answer is *yes*, then no change in the grading process is needed and the student should be graded as any other student in the class. For grade-level expectations that are not likely to be achieved during the academic year without special services and supports, the team should move to Step 2.

STEP 2. DETERMINE WHETHER AN ACCOMMODATION OR MODIFICATION IS NEEDED

For each grade-level expectation or standard that requires support or adaptation, the educational team asks whether an accommodation or a modification is needed. If the team determines that only accommodations are needed, then no change in the grading process is needed. A student who takes a social studies test orally, for example, should be graded based on the content of his or her responses with no penalty for the accommodation. If modifications are deemed necessary, however, then teams go through the remaining three steps of the model for this expectation.

STEP 3. ESTABLISH THE APPROPRIATE CRITERIA FOR EACH AREA REQUIRING MODIFICATION

The third step is to determine the appropriate criteria for those expectations requiring modification. This modified expectation is what the team believes could reasonably be achieved by the end of the academic year with special supports. Defining the appropriate expectations does not imply different content, but rather implies criteria within that content area that are adjusted to an achievable level for the student. Modified expectations are recorded goals on the individualized education program (IEP), Section 504 plan, or English learner (EL) plan, along with other goals the student may need for success in daily classroom routines.

STEP 4. GRADE BASED ON THE MODIFIED STANDARD.

For areas in which modifications are needed, grades should be based on the modified expectations instead of the grade-level expectations. There is no need to report a failing grade on the grade-level expectation. A failing grade would not be new information. Nor would it be fair or meaningful to simply add points for effort or behavior. Instead, the student should be graded on the criteria the team determined were appropriate. If an *A* means *mastered* for all students, and an exceptional learner masters the modified expectation, then the student has earned an *A*.

STEP 5. COMMUNICATE THE MEANING OF THE GRADE.

The final step in the process is to provide additional information to explain grades for modified expectations. Assigning grades that are based on modified expectations without

Figure 30.1 Inclusive Grading Model

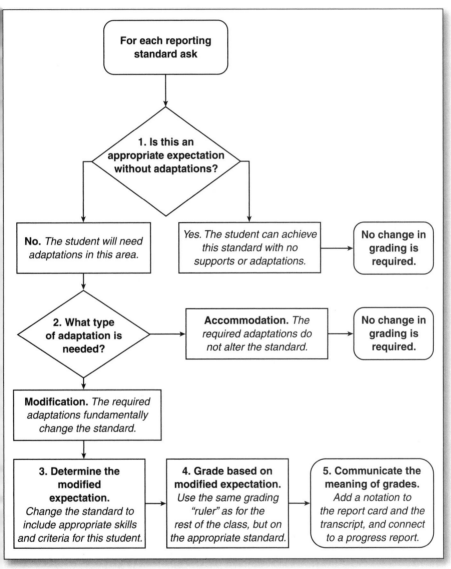

Source: Jung & Guskey (2010).

communicating what was truly measured is no more meaningful or fair than giving failing grades based on grade-level expectations. In this last essential step, teachers note which grades were based on different criteria. The report card

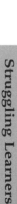

should include a special notation, such as an asterisk, beside grades that reflect achievement on modified standards. The accompanying footnote might be worded, *based on modified expectations.* Additional description on the report card can direct families to a supplemental progress report that includes the standards on which the grade was based and progress data. This lets everyone know how the student performed, but that the performance was based on a modified expectation.

REFERENCES

Bursuck, W. D., Munk, D. D., & Olson, M. M. (1999). The fairness of report card grading adaptations: What do students with and without disabilities think? *Remedial and Special Education, 20,* 84–92.

Donahue, K., & Zigmond, N. (1990). Academic grades of ninth-grade urban learning disabled students and low-achieving peers. *Exceptionality, 1*(1), 17–27.

Jung, L. A., (2009). The challenges of grading and reporting in special education: An inclusive grading model. In T. R. Guskey (Ed.), *Practical solutions for serious problems in standards-based grading* (pp. 27–40). Thousand Oaks, CA: Corwin.

Jung, L. A., & Guskey, T. R. (2010). Grading exceptional learners. *Educational Leadership, 67*(5), 31–35.

Jung, L. A., & Guskey, T. R. (2007). Standards-based grading and reporting: A model for special education. *Teaching Exceptional Children, 40*(2), 48–53.

Jung, L. A., & Guskey, T. R. (2012). *Grading exceptional and struggling learners.* Thousand Oaks, CA: Corwin.

Polloway, E. A., Epstein, M. H., Bursuck, W. D., Roderique, T. W., McConeghy, J. L., & Jayanthi, M. (1994). Classroom grading: A national survey of policies. *Remedial and Special Education, 15,* 162–170.

Ring, M. M., & Reetz, L. (2000). Modification effects on attribution of middle school students with learning disabilities. *Learning Disabilities Research and Practice, 15,* 34–42.

Silva, M., Munk, D. D., & Bursuck, W. D. (2005). Grading adaptations for students with disabilities. *Intervention in School and Clinic, 41,* 87–98.

31

What Is the Difference Between *Accommodations* and *Modifications?*

B ecause determining the appropriate grade for exceptional learners hinges upon determining the accommodations and modifications needed, it is important for all teachers to have a clear understanding of the difference between the two. Although accommodations and modifications are adaptations to the curriculum, they function in very different ways. This difference in function has important implications for progress monitoring and grading.

ACCOMMODATIONS

In basic terms, accommodations simply allow students to participate fully in the instructional program. They can be thought of as similar to eyeglasses. A student who needs eyeglasses in order to see well is permitted to wear them in the classroom at all times. The eyeglasses simply give the student access to the material. They do not make the material easier for that student than for any one else in the classroom.

Rather, they allow the students to participate as fully as students who have better vision. In essence, eyeglasses simply "level the playing field" (Freedman, 2005a, p. 47) for that student. Accommodations serve in exactly the same way. Accommodations are *supports that provide access to the general curriculum but do not fundamentally alter the learning goal or grade-level standard* (Freedman, 2000, 2005a).

MODIFICATIONS

For some students, however, an accommodation is not enough. These students need additional support in certain areas in order to be successful. In considering the educational background and learning history of these students, the educational team might decide that some or all of the grade-level standards are not achievable during the academic year and some change or *modification* in the standards is needed. Unlike accommodations that simply level the playing field, modifications actually "change the game" (Freedman, 2005a, p. 48). Modifications are *changes to the curriculum and assessments that do fundamentally alter the learning goal or grade-level expectation* (Freedman, 2000, 2005a, 2005b).

DIFFERENCES IN FUNCTION

From the definitions above, it would seem that we could construct a list of possible adaptations and then categorize each as an accommodation or a modification. Many schools, as well as numerous textbooks, websites, and articles, do exactly this. These lists of possible adaptations almost always consider *extended time* and *oral test taking* to be accommodations. But what many educators do not recognize is that these popular adaptations may or *may not* be an accommodation. We cannot determine the function of the adaptation unless we know what is being measured. Because of this, few adaptations can be labeled as always an accommodation or a modification. Let us consider five common adaptations and their functions:

1. Offer Extended Time

One of the most common adaptations is to offer extended time on an assessment or to complete an assignment. If the purpose of the assessment is to measure students' knowledge and understanding of particular concepts and not to measure speed or response rate, then extended time is an *accommodation*. And, indeed, the purpose of most assessments and assignments is to determine students' mastery of content or to provide evidence of a learning process, not to measure students' speed or rate of performance.

There are, however, instances when extended time is clearly a modification. One of those instances is if the assessment is specifically designed to measure students' speed or rate of performance. In certain math or reading assignments, such as "Mad Minutes" in mathematics and timed reading, for example, the provision of extra time would be considered a *modification*, because both accuracy *and* rate of performance are being measured. Similar examples can be found in keyboarding and physical education.

2. Complete a Task Orally

Allowing a student to take quizzes or exams orally is also a common adaptation for struggling learners. This adaptation is a great choice for students whose verbal skills are much higher than their writing skills, a scenario common to English language learners and students with learning disabilities. Taking an assessment orally is an *accommodation* for any assessment that is not designed to measure proficiency in writing. If the assessment is connected to a grade or mark on a writing standard, however, it is a *modification*.

3. Use Computerized Spell, Grammar, and Punctuation Check

For students who struggle with the conventions of spelling, grammar, and punctuation in writing, the use of computerized word processors can serve as an excellent accommodation. As

Struggling Learners

they work to complete written assignments, these students can concentrate on demonstrating fully what they have learned and are able to do, knowing that a prompt will be given for many of the spelling, grammar, and punctuation errors they might have. This use of computerized spelling, grammar, and punctuation checks is an *accommodation* for any assessment or assignment not connected to a grade or mark in conventions of writing. In subjects such as mathematics, science, or social studies, for example, the assessments are generally designed to measure students' understanding of concepts in those subjects, not their writing ability. To use word processing software to complete assignments in such subjects is an accommodation. On the other hand, this same adaptation would be considered a *modification* if the assessment or assignment focuses on language arts standards and is designed to measure students' proficiency in the conventions of writing.

4. Complete Only Certain Parts of the Task or Answer Fewer Questions

Reducing the length of assessments or assignments is an adaptation frequently chosen for struggling learners and for those who require additional time to complete tasks. This adaptation may mean fewer questions, problems, or tasks. And as is true of most adaptations, this can function as either an accommodation or a modification.

If all parts of the assignment address the same standard(s), and the length of the assignment is designed to provide more practice, then eliminating portions of the assignment is an accommodation. For example, a teacher might adapt an assignment of 100, two-digit multiplication problems by requiring that a struggling learner completes only 50. This adaptation is considered an *accommodation* as long as all 100 problems are of comparable difficulty and measure the same skill. Instead of extending the time allowed, the redundancy in the task is eliminated.

Reducing the length of an assessments or assignment becomes a *modification*, however, when more difficult parts of the assessment or assignment are not required. A mathematics teacher, for example, may adapt an assignment by requiring that a student complete all of the two-digit multiplication problems, but none of the three-digit ones. By taking away the more difficult items from the task, the assignment has been modified.

5. Offer a Take-Home Task Instead of an In-Class Task

Having students complete a task in class can be the perfect way for a teacher to quickly check students' understanding of a concept and then offer immediate feedback. But for some struggling learners, the time constraints of the class period or the pressure of completing the assignment in the same way or at the same speed as others in the class can be difficult to manage. In these circumstances, an educational team may decide to allow the student to complete certain assessments or assignments at home instead of in class. This adaptation is an *accommodation* if, and only if, all of the same relevant resources are available to the student at home as are available to students completing it in class. On the other hand, if students taking a quiz in class are not permitted to use Internet resources, books, or class notes that are available to the student completing it at home, then this adaptation is a *modification*.

REFERENCES

Freedman, M. K. (2000). *Testing, grading and granting diplomas to special education students: Individuals with Disabilities Education Law Report—Special Report No. 18.* Horsham, PA: LRP Publications.

Freedman, M. K. (2005a). *Student testing and the law: The requirements educators, parents, and officials should know.* Horsham, PA: LRP Publications.

Freedman, M. K. (2005b). *Grades, report cards, etc. . . . and the law.* Boston, MA: School Law Pro.

Struggling Learners

32

How Do We Legally Report Grades for Exceptional and Struggling Learners on Report Cards and Transcripts?

The issue of failing grades for exceptional and struggling learners is a difficult topic that many districts avoid by simply disallowing failing grades for students with IEPs. However, from a legal perspective, any student—exceptional or otherwise—can receive a failing grade on an assignment or an assessment, or in a subject area or course. The important distinction with exceptional learners is why the failure occurred. Legal provisions stipulate that individual education programs (IEPs) must provide students with disabilities the opportunity to receive passing grades and advance in grade level with their peers (Board of Education v. Rowley, 1982). This litigation yielded two important implications for schools. First, no student may fail because needed services were not provided. If a student with a disability or an English learner (EL) fails a subject or class, the school must be prepared to demonstrate that appropriate supports were provided. Otherwise, a failing grade may be seen as an indication of failure on the part of the school, not as the students' failure (Board of Education v. Rowley, 1982).

Second, a student should not fail on a standard that the education team determined was unattainable for that student. Instead, individualized goals should be written in the IEP, Section 504 plan, or EL plan based on the level of work the student is able to complete successfully. If, however, appropriate services and supports are in place and the appropriate level of work is assessed, then the same range of grades available to all students is applicable to exceptional and struggling learners, including failing grades. The key is to be clear that the grade is based on appropriate expectations for the student, and to have evidence to support the accuracy and appropriateness of the grade assigned.

REPORT CARDS AND TRANSCRIPTS

Perhaps the most common of all reporting myths is that modifications cannot be noted on any student's report card or transcript. First, it is important to understand the legal distinction between report cards and transcripts, or permanent records. The U.S. Department of Education's Office of Civil Rights (OCR) sees the purpose of report cards to communicate information about students' achievement with *the students and parents,* and whoever parents and students give permission to see them. Because report cards are not consumed by a third party, teachers and schools can *legally* include any information they like about a student's modified program and even eligibility for special education. Notice that we say that teachers can *legally* include eligibility status, rather than we recommend that they do. This information would unlikely ever be needed, but it is not illegal to include it.

Transcripts are a different matter. The OCR acknowledges that transcripts are indeed shared with other schools, with employers, and with institutes of higher education. Because of third-party sharing, rules of confidentiality apply to transcripts that do not apply to report cards. Under the Individuals with Disabilities Education Act (IDEA) of 1997 and the Individuals with Disabilities Education Improvement Act (2004), Section 504 of the Rehabilitation Act of 1973, and the Americans with Disabilities Act Amendments Act of 2008, transcripts cannot identify students as having a disability. Therefore, we cannot include words like *IEP* or *Special Education* on the transcript. However, noting a *modified* curriculum *is* legal, as long as modifications are available to any student who needs them. In other words, if modifications are available to students with disabilities, English learners, and other exceptional or struggling students, then noting that a course grade is based on modified expectations is legal, and a practice we recommend (Jung & Guskey, 2012).

Schools using standards-based report cards *always base overall, summary grades or marks on the most recent evidence,* never on an average of marks across marking periods. The purpose of standards-based grading is to reflect accurately what students have learned and are able to do at a specific point in time. The permanent records or transcripts of exceptional and struggling learners are much the same. The only difference would be the designation of grades or marks that have been based on modified standards. To indicate that a modification was made to the standards recorded in permanent records or transcripts is legal (Office of Civil Rights, 2008). It also enhances the accuracy and honesty of the included information.

REFERENCES

Board of Education v. Rowley, 458 U.S. 176 (1982).

Individuals with Disabilities Education Improvement Act (IDEIA), 20 U.S.C. §§ 1400 to 1482 (2004).

Jung, L. A., & Guskey, T. R. (2012). *Grading exceptional and struggling learners.* Thousand Oaks, CA: Corwin.

Office of Civil Rights. (2008, October 17). *Dear colleague letter: Report cards and transcripts for students with disabilities.* Available at http://www.ed.gov/about/offices/list/ocr/letters/colleague-20081017.html

Rehabilitation Act of 1973, 29 U.S.C. 794 § 504.

33

Do High School Students Requiring Modifications Receive Course Credit Toward a Diploma? Do Modifications Make a Student Ineligible for Extracurricular Activities, Such as Interscholastic Athletics?

Although all educators face the challenge of determining how to grade exceptional learners, secondary educators face decisions in several areas of policy. Specifically, they must consider issues related to granting course credit, calculating a grade-point average (GPA), and determining eligibility for extracurricular activities. There are numerous legal ways to answer questions about each of these topics. The key to success (and legality) in each of these areas rests in determining policy that is communicated clearly to students and families, and then implemented consistently. Below we highlight the most immediate questions school leaders will need to address.

COURSE CREDIT

Decisions on course credit are the first that secondary schools must make in order to implement fair and appropriate grading policies. The essential question is, "To what extent can expectations be modified and a student still receive credit for the course?" For some students, only one, relatively minor area of the course may require modification. For others, modifications may be needed for nearly all of the course standards.

The heart of the question about course credit lies in where to draw the line. Some schools may decide that if any standard is modified, course credit is not granted. Others may craft a formula for modifications or a list of minimum criteria that students must meet. Another option is to develop a process for considering students individually. In other schools, the decision may rest solely on students' performance on required end-of-course exams.

For students with disabilities, the decisions schools make about course credit will affect decisions students make with their families during individualized education program (IEP) meetings. A student may wish to attempt to pass course requirements, even if entitled to modifications, if that impacts whether course credit is granted or a diploma is earned.

GRADE-POINT AVERAGE (GPA)

Calculating the GPA is a second major decision secondary school leaders will face. The question is, "How will a student's GPA be determined when some grades are based on modified expectations?" Schools may decide not to include any grades based on modifications in the calculation. Or, schools may include all grades but place an asterisk or other mark by the

GPA to indicate some grades were based on different criteria. Still another option is to reduce the amount of credit given for grades based on modifications. Clearly, each of these options offers a range of positive and negative consequences.

ELIGIBILITY FOR EXTRACURRICULAR ACTIVITIES

Another related issue for secondary schools involved in inclusive grading is eligibility for extracurricular activities. In particular, participation in athletics is an area that requires careful consideration as school leaders determine policies for modified expectations. Students who need to spend additional time on academics to catch up may be hampered in their progress if they devote many hours to a sport. At the same time, a school certainly does not want to deny students with disabilities or English learners access to participation in athletics, especially when such participation might be the *only* time at school that some students do not feel the effects of their disability. For some struggling students, athletics may be their first school success. Such participation in athletics also can foster stronger school affiliation. So no matter what strategy is chosen for determining GPA, the academic requirements for athletic eligibility should be based on students' performance on expectations considered appropriate for their ability. (For additional reading on this topic, see Jung & Guskey, 2011, 2112).

REFERENCES

Jung, L. A., & Guskey, T. R. (2011). Fair and accurate grading for exceptional learners. *Principal Leadership, 12*(3), 32–37.

Jung, L. A., & Guskey, T. R. (2012). *Grading exceptional and struggling learners.* Thousand Oaks, CA: Corwin.

Struggling Learners

Summary and Conclusions

The challenges associated with education reforms regarding standards, assessments, grading, and reporting are many and complex. These challenges test the will and determination of the most dedicated educators. But while serious and daunting, these challenges are not insurmountable. Meeting them requires a firm understanding of the knowledge base in each area, the courage to challenge long-held traditions, and a strong and abiding commitment to doing what is truly best for students at every level of education.

We've tried our best in this book to offer that necessary understanding of our knowledge base in each of these important areas. We've also tried to describe guidelines stemming from that knowledge base for improving practice. As we noted many times, much of what is written about these topics is based more on opinion and conjecture, rather than on valid evidence of what is most honest and effective. Hopefully we have provided a useful summary of that evidence when it exists and offered helpful suggestions on how it can used to develop better policies and practices. The necessary courage and commitment, however, must come from you.

We remain convinced the only way to reduce the gap between our knowledge base and practice is to question those long-held traditions and to push hard for practices known to be more effective. If our answers to these essential questions and the accompanying ideas we presented aid in improvement initiatives and inspire commitment among educators at all levels to do better, then we will consider our efforts a success.

Index